MISSION-
READY
Marriage

MISSION-READY
Marriage

---⭐---

A CHRISTIAN GUIDE TO DISCOVERING HOPE AND PURPOSE AS A MILITARY WIFE

ASHLEY ASHCRAFT

B&H
PUBLISHING®
BRENTWOOD, TENNESSEE

978-1-4300-8975-9

Published by B&H Publishing Group
Brentwood, Tennessee

Dewey Decimal Classification: 306.81
Subject Heading: MISSIONS / MARRIAGE / MILITARY
PERSONNEL

Cover design by B&H Publishing Group.
Illustration by Olha Turchenko/Shutterstock; star image by sharpner/Shutterstock. Author photo by Courtney Mitchell.

1 2 3 4 5 6 • 27 26 25 24

To *every* military spouse (past, present, and future),
Thank you for the integral and sacrificial
role you play in service to our nation.

To Tim,
Thank you for praying for me to fall in love
with Jesus and embracing the vulnerable task
of sharing our marriage with the world!

To Wally and Bunnie,
Thank you for showing Tim and me what it looks like to be
a military husband and wife team after God's own heart.

Acknowledgments

God, thank You for Your unwavering grace and love and for continuing to speak truth into my life daily through Your living Word. I praise You for Your supreme investment in marriage. Although marriage is often challenging, with You as the center, there is unlimited hope and joy to be discovered and rediscovered.

Tim, we have been *through* it, facing challenges and trials we never could have fathomed. But our faith in Jesus and our commitment to one another keep us united. Thank you for taking the kids on adventures every Saturday, which gave me dedicated time to write. You are my "Forever Love."

Adeline, Lincoln, Isla, and Finley, you are my precious gifts from the Lord. I pray the marriage you see up close each day points you to Jesus, both in how we forgive and how we love. Thank you for understanding when I needed time to work on this project. P.S. You are each exceptional storytellers.

Dad, Mom, Travis, and Brooke, thank you for encouraging my desire to write and faithfully helping our family through every step of this military journey.

Dave, Joan, Chris, and Amy, I am immeasurably grateful for your love and assistance through each season, celebration, and challenge the military presents.

Jennifer, Kelly, Mandy, Kim, Lisa, Meredith, and Savanah, thank you for praying for me, offering advice, cheering me on, and holding me accountable. And to all the women scattered across the globe who feel like family, I could write a book about how special you are to me!

My Bible study group (Sarah, Rachel, Erin, Angela, and Amber), you prayed this book into existence! Thank you for your weekly encouragement, example, and sisterhood.

My writing prayer team (Erin, Angela, and Amber), you walked through every stage of this with me and went to war in daily prayer. I am forever grateful.

My beta reader team, you drastically improved the message within these pages with your thoughtful feedback and ideas. Thank you for making this book more relevant.

Megan Brown, you are a fierce gift to our military community. Thank you for illuminating my role as a military spouse and guiding me as a writer.

Pastor Andrew Taylor, you helped shape the contents of this book through your feedback about pastoring military families and your weekly sermons. Thank you for faithfully shepherding Liberty Church and praying for this project.

My agent, Dan Balow, thank you for taking a chance on me and using your expertise to help bring this project to fruition. Your faith, kindness, and wisdom inspire me.

My editor, Ashley Gorman, you have a beautiful gift for seeing into a reader's heart and knowing how to love them well through words. Thank you for identifying the gaps and filling them in with truth. You added the drizzle of honey each chapter needed.

The team at B&H, thank you for entertaining all my ideas, enabling me to be a voice behind the scenes, and helping this book come to life. To Jade and Susan, thank you for all your work on the cover. To Kim, thank you for your expertise in book production. And to Ashley V., thank you for your diligence in marketing!

Jesse and Leah Roberts (of Poor Bishop Hooper), your music kept me company with each word I typed. Thank you for your dedication to glorifying God through song.

Contents

Chapter One

Sacrifice: A Look at God's Rescue Plan on the Battlefield

The most significant sacrifice
I've made as a military spouse
was _____.

When I married my husband inside the granite walls of a hundred-year-old chapel in New York, I had no idea what I was getting myself into as a military spouse. No one who had previously walked this well-worn path explained the sacrificial life I agreed to when I said "I do" to a service member. Yet it took only a couple of days to discover the truth.

The first sacrifice came when the Army denied our request for a honeymoon. After our wedding, my husband was granted *two days of leave* before reporting to his new position at Fort Cavazos, Texas (formerly Fort Hood), in an Apache helicopter unit. His long nights at work and frequent absence on the weekends confirmed this sacrificial lifestyle.

A Matter of Life and Death

One month before we were to celebrate our first wedding anniversary, the Army decided it was the perfect time to send my husband away. On a scorching Texas summer afternoon, I kissed Tim goodbye in an empty parking lot. The Army sent him 7,460 miles away to fight the Global War on Terror in Afghanistan.

So on July 25, I spent our anniversary alone, watching reality television on an ugly, brown suede couch my husband and his former roommate picked up at a local furniture store in Alabama.

Thirty-four days later, while I sat on our shaggy maroon rug grading high school English essays, the phone rang. A Maryland phone number showed up on the screen, and I knew that meant my husband was making his daily call from Forward Operating Base Salerno, Afghanistan.

"Hey, Babe!" I was so excited to hear his voice I stood.

Silence.

"Babe?"

As Tim remained quiet, goose bumps rose on my arms.

"I'm okay, but our helicopter got shot down this morning."

I fell to my knees near our glass coffee table. Other than having two uniformed Soldiers standing on my doorstep, informing me of my husband's death, this was the next most terrifying event I could imagine.

"What?! Are you okay?" I didn't know what to think. All my pre-deployment training vanished from my brain.

"Yes, I'm okay."

"Are you sure? You didn't get injured anywhere?"

"No, a couple of rounds went through my cockpit near my legs, but they missed me."

"What happened?"

"About 150 insurgents dressed in stolen U.S. military uniforms attacked our base, and a couple dozen started to breach the wire."

"Are you allowed to be telling me this? Will you get in trouble?" I asked, remembering our pre-deployment training about operational security.

"It's fine."

"I can't believe this! Is the other pilot okay? Who were our flying with?"

"I was flying with Jake Marceaux. We had just landed when insurgents attacked the base, and we decided to launch again. Fifteen bullets pierced the helicopter, some barely missed my legs, and another grazed Jake's shoulder, miraculously missing his neck."

He paused again.

"It's the month of Ramadan, and today is known as the Night of Power. The extremists believe that if they kill us today, Allah will reward them a thousandfold in heaven."

My stomach lurched at his words.

"We only survived by the grace of God. A rocket-propelled grenade missed the nose of the aircraft by one foot. I thought that was going to be it."

My breath seemed to stop as the images sprang to life in my mind. And then deep concern set in for my husband's emotional state in the aftermath of the attack.

"Were you scared?"

"I was at peace because I felt God's presence. But there wasn't time to be scared because we were literally fighting for our lives. We have to go debrief now. There's a lot to do here. I love you."

"I love you too, Babe! Be safe!"

I made it through the phone call without breaking down, still too shocked to process the trauma of what just happened to the man I desperately loved. I immediately called my parents in Arizona, and my tears finally emerged in blubbering sobs of fear. Tim still had ten months to go in Afghanistan.

The sacrifice of this military life took on a new meaning after that phone call. We were not just missing honeymoons and wedding anniversaries. This was a matter of *life and death*. The next ten months proved that true as Tim regularly flew operational missions in the most dangerous valleys in Afghanistan. And right as we started making our patriotic homecoming banners back in Texas, a Soldier in Tim's platoon, Chris Thibodeau, died after his Apache went down responding to an enemy attack on another base. There was no longer any way to romanticize this lifestyle.

God Works in Our Loneliness

When my husband returned home, it quickly became apparent that we were two selfish and naive twenty-six-year-olds ill-equipped to reintegrate our lives after the traumatic effects of war. Throw in a military move two weeks later for a six-month course at Fort Novosel, Alabama (formerly Fort Rucker), and despite the fact that we genuinely cherished each other, we were a mess. Thankfully, our priority after every move is immediately plugging into a local church. That priority saved us.

Two years before this move, I surrendered my life to God and accepted Jesus as my Savior while soaking in the bathtub and reading Max Lucado's *3:16: The Numbers of Hope*. In this book, Lucado thoroughly explains one verse, John 3:16, which states: "For God loved the world in this way: He gave his one and only Son, so that everyone who believes in him will not perish but have eternal life." The author's explanation of God's Word opened my eyes to the truth of Jesus's divine identity and gospel work on my behalf.

When Tim returned from Afghanistan, I was still a new Christian with *very little* knowledge of what it meant to live according to the Scriptures. In fact, I believed the goal of marriage was happiness and, really, *my* happiness. If you married for happiness too, you know it doesn't take long for life to blow up that idea.

Once I accepted Christ, I attended church regularly and participated in weekly Bible studies, but God was not the foundation of my life yet. Instead, I placed my extremely impressive, all-American, win-every-award, play-every-instrument, MVP husband on God's throne. And thankfully, though painfully, God was about to take His rightful place in my life.

As we settled into our tiny 1940s home in the heart of downtown Enterprise, Alabama, loneliness moved in, and I began to question my purpose while sitting at home by myself. Here I was, jobless in a small town after receiving a teaching award in our nation's capital two months prior. I was also friendless and familyless. And the effects of a traumatic war experience made me feel like I also lost my husband. I felt like God stripped me of everything and everyone I loved. I was officially *un*happy.

I turned to the church with nothing to occupy my time during my husband's six-month course. On Wednesday mornings, I attended a women's Bible study to discuss Charles F. Stanley's book *When the Enemy Strikes*, which taught me about Satan's tactics to destroy our lives—knowledge I desperately needed. Next, our church posed a seemingly absurd challenge: read the entire Bible in ninety days. With no job, I had no excuse not to do it. So I joined the challenge and embarked on a journey that would dramatically change my life.

Armed with a handful of crayons to highlight my Bible (something I witnessed from my husband's time with a Christian group called Navigators), my reading plan, and a pen, I waded and stumbled through the sixty-six books of the Bible. I had no training on how to study it. I did not understand the historical and cultural contexts. I had no clue how to pronounce all the names and cities listed. And my mind was littered with questions. Yet I read it with the faithful help of the Holy Spirit. In John 14:26, God promises us that "the Counselor, the Holy

Spirit, whom the Father will send in my name, will teach you all things and remind you of everything I have told you." Like all God's promises, this one held true.

I didn't complete the challenge in ninety days but persevered and finished in 150. Those days in the Scriptures, read while sitting in the shade of our pecan tree out back or curled up on that same brown sofa, softened my heart and transformed my mind. They provided me with hope and trust in God during a time when life felt out of control. They taught me how to love my husband sincerely and sacrificially. God's Word showed me that this life is not about me and my worldly happiness. He placed me here to love Him and love others.

Fast-forward a decade, and I now know that God works in mysterious and often uncomfortable ways to get our attention and bring our broken selves to Him. Looking back, I am thankful for the season of loneliness God provided in Alabama, which led me to an intimate relationship with Him. The Lord had to bring me to a quiet place to reorder my priorities and lead me to the abundant life He planned for me. And the military is part of that plan.

The Ultimate Sacrifice

Although God used the circumstances of the military to deepen my relationship with Him, no military resources or training will completely equip us to handle this lifestyle healthily. But there is Somebody who will: Jesus Christ. I learned that the hard way. As we live a lifestyle of turmoil and sacrifice, we can only experience hope and peace through the One who made the ultimate sacrifice.

Of all people, I do not have to tell you that we live in a broken, sin-soaked world filled with selfishness and evil. Service members and their spouses see this daily as they strive to protect our freedoms against all enemies, foreign and domestic. But a sin-filled world was not God's original plan for us. If we explore the first two chapters of the Bible, we find that Genesis 1–2 reveals a safe, peaceful, and beautiful world that God called "good." No violence, no selfishness, no evil.

Unfortunately, like you and me, the first man and woman (Adam and Eve) were not content with this peaceful world God provided. Instead, as we read Genesis 3 and beyond, we find that they listened to Satan's twisted words and decided to disobey God's command not to eat from the tree of knowledge of good and evil. That act of disobedience separated humanity from God forever.

Militarily speaking, Adam and Eve's transgression against God's rule would be akin to your husband being in battle on foreign soil and disobeying his commander's orders. Imagine that your husband's disobedience leads him to be separated from his commander and taken captive by the enemy. The commander would refuse to leave your husband behind, despite his negligence. In pursuit of his survival, the commander would devise a special operation to rescue him, knowing one of his own would have to perish to save your husband.

In essence, that is what happened when God sacrificed His Son for us. Our inherent sin separated us from God, but He implemented a plan to save us from the enemy (and our own sin!) in His loving mercy. He willingly sent His one and only Son to the cross to pay the debt for our sins. Jesus's sacrifice on the cross wiped our sins clean, and as believers in Christ, God now sees us through the pure and filtered lens of Jesus. That means that if you are in Christ today, not only has your record of wrong been erased from the ledger, but the ledger is now filled back up with a record of perfect obedience—*Christ's* obedience. God now sees you as standing on Jesus's record instead of your own, and in Christ's record you're completely covered. (If this message is new to you, or you haven't decided to stand on Christ's record instead of your own, let me encourage you—now is the moment to choose it for yourself!)

Christ's death on the cross also calls us to lead a life of sacrifice. We must die to our selfish wishes and whims to honor and glorify the Father as faithful followers of Jesus. Though it sounds counterintuitive, the true key to a successful life and marriage requires a willingness to surrender our deepest desires to the will of our Father—something I failed at for years.

God's Plan Is Better Than Ours

I openly struggled with resentment and discontent for almost a decade after the enemy shot down Tim's helicopter. I yearned for the stereotypical all-American dream, white picket fence and all. I wanted to live in Arizona, raising my kids with our extended family. I wanted stability. I wanted my husband at the dinner table every night. I wanted Tim to be home to kiss our children good night and have breakfast with them in the morning. I wanted him to be present for all our family's activities, birthdays, holidays, and anniversaries. I wanted the freedom to go on mission trips worldwide and plan vacations more than a week in advance.

But God had a different plan. To fulfill God's Great Commission of sharing Jesus, He placed our family in the military. This time in my life is not the season for me to serve in Africa or Mexico. God needs me to serve in the military community right now, loving service members and their families. He placed me here to learn (repeatedly!) to die to myself and how to sacrifice my selfish desires for my husband, my children, my country, and my God.

Everything I just said probably sounds like doomsday to you—as if the only feeling you can expect will be pain as you give up your own plans for the sake of others. But a funny thing happens when you start living this way—not just in military contexts but every context. You start experiencing intimacy and joy. You start experiencing that deep peace our world was always made for. You see, *God is bigger than the white picket fence,* and His plans for your marriage are far grander than yours. If you partner with God to accomplish His goals for your marriage, just watch what He will do! Saying yes to God's plan for your marriage is a rewarding and eternal adventure I cannot wait for you to start.

But please note you are *not* in control of your husband, his choices in your marriage, or his faith. You are only in charge of yourself. Do you know how I know? I tried controlling my husband for years, and honestly, it's something I still struggle with. As you read this book, continually *pray* for your husband, asking God to draw your husband intimately close to his Creator and giving him the desire to surrender his life fully to Jesus. God can work through us to influence our husbands, but *He* is the one who offers the gift of salvation and guides our husbands' hearts through the Holy Spirit. I pray that gives you permission to relax and let the Lord do the heavy lifting.

Through this book, I plan to prepare you practically and spiritually to live a God-honoring, gospel-centered, mission-minded, joy-filled marriage from your husband's first oath through his farewell ceremony and beyond. With that goal in mind, I prayed that the Lord's words would come through my fingertips each time I sat down to write for you. I earnestly prayed that He would lead every chapter of this book, understanding that only He knows the hearts of every person who will read this book.

I can't possibly speak to every spousal experience in the military, but through my experiences and some of those shared by my friends, I pray the Lord speaks to you. Through these words, may you know God's heart, hear His voice, experience His love, and feel emboldened to fulfill your call as a military wife.

Finally, this book was written for you whether you believe in Jesus, desire to know Him, have never heard of Him, or deny His existence (that used to be me). Come as you are!

Prayer

Dear God,

You know my heart as I begin this book. You are not surprised by my beliefs, my doubts, my attitudes, my fears, or my thoughts. You know them all before I even think them. And yet, You love me anyway. Heavenly Father, through these pages, please open my eyes to see You and what You're doing through my military marriage. Reveal Your goodness, mercy, and love to me. Help me understand that my sacrifices as a military wife are not in vain. Show me why You've placed me here, Lord. I'm ready. In Jesus's hope-filled name, amen.

───────── *Reflection Questions* ─────────

1. Do you believe there's a reason why you're in the military community? Explain.

2. What was one of the first sacrifices you made as a new military wife?

3. How has loneliness been a part of your military spouse journey?

4. Is reading the Bible a part of your life?

5. What questions do you have about your faith, the Bible, or Jesus?

6. Was marrying a military man something you envisioned for your life?

───────── *Next Steps* ─────────

- ❑ Commit to having an open mind as you read through this book.
- ❑ Invite a friend or group to read along with you.

───────── *Resources* ─────────

For links and descriptions of each resource, visit Ashleyashcraft.com/missionreadymarriage.

- *Never Alone* by Jessica Manfre, LMSW

- *Know What You Signed Up For* by Megan B. Brown
- *Brave Women, Strong Faith* compiled by Megan B. Brown
- *You Are Not Alone* by Jen McDonald
- *God Strong* by Sara Horn

Chapter Two

Marriage: The Purpose and the Gift

When I first got married, I thought
_____ was the goal of
marriage.

On a chilly New Year's Eve in Destin, Florida, ninety miles southwest of the Army's flight school at Fort Novosel, Alabama, Tim leaped over crashing waves to retrieve a seashell worthy of braving the cold December waters. I couldn't believe what he pulled out of that turquoise ocean. It was a perfectly formed clamshell the size of a baseball, cream-colored with hints of burnt orange on the tips. And that's when he dropped to one knee on the white, powdery beach, revealing a diamond ring within the shell.

When I said yes to Tim's marriage proposal at age twenty-three, I had only a minimal understanding of God's design for marriage. It was just a few months before he got down on one knee that I even desired to open the Bible. On that sunset-lit beach in Florida, I thought a successful marriage equated to personal happiness—mostly mine.

It took me about ten years of marriage to learn that judging a marriage's quality based on how happy it makes you is a complete setup by the enemy. You struggle with sin, and your husband struggles with sin. And while there is much more to your Christian identity than just being a sinner, the truth is that when two sin-strugglers marry each other, they are inevitably going to do things that upset each other, disrupting your feelings of happiness. There's hope, though. Through practice and maturity, believers in Christ experience unexplainable peace and contentment, even when marriage isn't going perfectly. Those emotions run deeper than happiness and only come from a heart transformed by God.

Unfortunately, we have a very real and conniving enemy, and he goes by the name Satan. (We'll talk more about him in chapter 4.) Suppose he can get you to view your marriage as "unhappy." Discontentment is like the bits of smoldering wood in a fireplace. Focusing on marital displeasure is like letting somebody scoop hot embers from your fireplace and scatter them all over your house. It's only a matter of time before an ember starts a fire that destroys your home. *Wouldn't life be easier if I hadn't married a man in the military? Why does my life always revolve around my husband's career? Why don't I ever get a say? Did I marry the wrong person?*

But here's some relief for you: *God has you where you are and who you're with for His purposes* (and for your blessing, believe it or not). You didn't marry the wrong person, and right now, you're not supposed to be in that place you think would make you happy. God determines your boundaries. Acts 17:26 assures us of this: "From one man he has made every nationality to live over the whole earth and has determined their appointed times and the boundaries of where they live."

Here's the tricky part: if you aren't perfectly pleased in your marriage, that's fine. None of us are happy all of the time in marriage. But, shockingly, your displeasure might be a significant part of God's plan for your spiritual growth. So let's delve into God's design for marriage.

Three Directions from the First Marriage

When God created the first man, Adam, He recognized that being alone was not good for him, so he lovingly created a "helper corresponding to him" (Gen. 2:18). Her name was Eve. The original Hebrew word for "helper" is *ezer*, which means one who gives material and spiritual assistance. As a helper, the role of a wife is to aid her husband in accomplishing the task God gave him. *The Moody Bible Commentary* explains that when God gave Adam the direction to "cultivate" and "keep" the land, those words denote worshipping/serving and obeying God.[1] Therefore, God designed us to help our husbands worship, serve, and obey our loving heavenly Father.

Also, the word *corresponding* comes from the Hebrew word *kenegdo*, which means "facing him" and implies looking at an image in the mirror.[2] We can envision Eve looking at Adam after God created her and seeing her reflection in Adam, both representing their Creator. We know this to be true because in Genesis 1:27 God states that He made both male *and* female in His image. Therefore, God does not view women as less important or worthy than men. They are a mirror image—equal.

Now, Adam and Eve started in a world different from our own. They began their partnership in the garden of Eden, a paradise free from anger, jealousy, shame, judgment, discontent, and deployments. God provided abundantly for them there, allowing Adam and Eve to eat from anywhere in the garden, minus one tree. They lived naked, feeling no concern over their bare bodies.

Sounds pretty good, right—frolicking around with your husband in a garden, naked and unashamed, without demands from Uncle Sam? Sign me up! However, the perfection didn't last. As we briefly explored in the last chapter, Eve and Adam fell for Satan's lies, doubting God and His goodness. They both ate from the one tree they were forbidden from eating, and in the aftermath, humans were forever separated from God by their inherited sin. Thankfully, God planned to send His Son, Jesus, to the world to restore our relationship with Him.

Before the fall (when Eve and Adam disobeyed the Lord), God gave us three intentions for marriage as seen in Genesis 2:24:

> "This is why a man **leaves** his father and mother and **bonds** with his wife, and they become **one flesh**." (emphasis added)

Let's look at each of these intentions briefly.

First, a man is to leave his father and mother. The fulfillment of the command to physically leave their parents is easy for most service members. Very few of them have the opportunity to live in their hometown while in the service unless in the reserve or guard. However, this also applies emotionally. A man needs to reorder his familial priorities once married and make his wife his primary confidant, not his parents. This is also true for the wife. After looking to God, we should look to our husbands for comfort and wisdom before confiding in our moms and dads.

Second, God says the husband is to bond with his wife. The meaning behind the word *bond* equates to an intentional and unbreakable commitment. *Merriam-Webster's Dictionary* defines *intention* as "the thing you plan to do or achieve: an aim or purpose."[3] Too many of us live out our marriages without a plan, aim, or purpose. I was undoubtedly guilty of this during the first decade of my marriage. Also, our culture is too quick to turn to divorce to resolve issues in marriage. As Jesus points in Matthew 5:32 (and other passages like Malachi 2:16 reveal), God designed marriage to be unbreakable. You don't need a definition there. God is clear.

Finally, Genesis 2 tells us that husband and wife are to become one flesh. *One flesh* means being totally united in *all* aspects of life—emotionally, spiritually, and physically. Mind, heart, and body, a husband and wife are now considered one unit as they walk through life together. Often, when we think "one flesh," we focus on the physical aspect, but it's important to remember it means more than just sexual intimacy. Still, let's explore that specific area of "one flesh."

God created sexual intimacy as a gift for married couples. Unfortunately, Satan works diligently to defile this beautiful blessing. He may have even tricked you into thinking it's wrong, burdensome, or disgusting. And tragically, many of us have experienced some form of sexual abuse that leaves us triggered in the bedroom. If that's you, I highly recommend a biblically and clinically informed counselor to help you process your pain and move toward healing and freedom.

It's easy to let sexual intimacy slip from the high place God put it when you're constantly packing up for your life, living in a state of upheaval, establishing a new home, sending your husband away, caring for children, changing your plans for the hundredth time due to the military, or _____ (insert your own reason here). We may even withhold physical intimacy because we're angry with this lifestyle and the constant sacrifices we have to make.

However, neglecting a God-honoring sex life is precisely what the enemy wants you to do. He intends to wedge you apart from your spouse by getting you to avoid regularly engaging in sexual intimacy. But are you ready for this truth? God actually desires for you to have an intoxicating sex life. In Proverbs 5, King Solomon warns his son against adultery, offering these words in verses 18–19: "Let your fountain be blessed, and rejoice in the wife of your youth, a lovely deer, a graceful doe. Let her breasts fill you at all times with delight; be intoxicated always in her love" (ESV). Isn't that amazing (and maybe a bit intimidating!)?

When we become one flesh with our husbands this way, we create a soul-level bond. Sexual intimacy recalibrates us. And that's something we need as military couples. So much of our military life keeps us apart that we have to fight intentionally to unite when we *are* together.

We've talked about God's three directions for marriage listed in Genesis—leaving, bonding, and becoming one flesh—but what is the actual *purpose* of marriage? What's the point, the big picture behind why He created man and woman to engage in marriage? Just as each of the sixty-six books of the Bible points us to Jesus, so does marriage.

Purpose One: Reconciliation

More than anything, our marriages are to reflect the gospel—a boots-on-the-ground visual of what it looks like to be sacrificially loved and forgiven even when we mess up. God wants each of our unions to look different from the world's picture of marriage. For example, the world says to look out for yourself. But God says to look out for your spouse. It's an entirely different way to do marriage. Paul explains this for us in Ephesians 5:22–32 when he tells believers a husband is supposed to represent Christ, loving his wife unconditionally and sacrificially for her benefit, and a wife is to symbolize the church, submitting herself to the loving care of her husband and, by extension, God, who looks out for her best interests.

The most important way we can reflect the love of Christ to the world through our marriages is by living a marriage of reconciliation. In this type of marriage, people recognize that significant others are sinful human beings who will fail them from time to time and sin daily. The failures and faults of our partners provide endless opportunities for us to practice forgiveness, patience, and love. Just as God does with us, when we repeatedly mess up.

When you live a marriage of reconciliation, you continually seek restoration with your spouse, and this regular pursuit helps show others the love of the Father. It's a real-world picture of the grace and mercy God offers through His Son's sacrifice on the cross, forgiving us when we don't deserve it, because He loves us. Is that a common practice in your marriage—regularly forgiving your spouse when he doesn't deserve it?

Purpose Two: Sanctification

Next, marriage is one of the most effective ways to move toward *sanctification,* a fancy word that means growing in your character to look more like Christ. God wants us to emit so much salt (truth) and light (joy) that others cannot help but see that there is something very different about us, and that difference is the hope we have in Jesus. Therefore, to look like Jesus, God provides lots of opportunities, experiences, and relationships to mold our character.

And what better relationship to shape you into Christlikeness than that of marriage?! The forced closeness of marriage creates the perfect scenario to constantly confront our inherently sinful nature: frustration, impatience, anger, malice, unforgiveness, self-righteousness, pride, shame, and so on. Every time we experience these negative emotions within ourselves and a spouse, there's an opportunity to become more like Christ (or less like Him). We get to choose if we will exhibit self-control, forgiveness, and patience or give in to how the enemy wants us to handle things.

The more a person chooses to work through emotions in a way that reflects the Savior's actions, the more that person spreads the gospel to their spouse and others. And I'm not sure there's another profession that stretches you more as a spouse than that of a service member. Day in and day out, we receive the opportunity to combat these hard and broken places of our hearts. Here are a few examples:

- Learning that your husband will deploy next month for the fifth time.

- A text that he can't make it home for dinner—again.
- The unit meeting informs you that your husband will be away at training for an entire month.
- When he misses your child's performance or game.
- Finding yourself next to an empty seat at church.
- Waking up with the baby at night with no help.
- Dealing with the inevitable broken appliances and car while he's away.
- Saying goodbye to your friends because he has orders to report to a new base.
- When he tells you the military denied his leave packet for Christmas.
- A sink full of dishes he can't empty.
- The barrage of work-related emails, texts, and phone calls that take his attention away from you.

I could go on for another ten pages, but I'll stop here. Each of these instances is an opportunity to recognize that our spouses in the service are not the enemy. We must submit our negative thoughts to the Lord and ask for His help to move toward reconciliation. We have to choose to lay down that cynical attitude that our flesh tells us we should rightfully parade around the house like a Macy's Thanksgiving Day balloon, letting it run into and bump against every wall, crevice, and person in our home.

But, if we consciously choose to puncture that balloon of discontent over time and with practice, it won't even have the chance to inflate. Insert sanctification.

I'm not saying it's wrong to feel sad or disappointed by these inevitable challenges. Of course we miss them (and their help!) when our husbands are far from home. Of course we feel a loss when we have to pack our boxes and leave friendships behind as we move to yet another city. Of course we want our children to have both parents at their major life events. And God is with us in our heartache, offering us strong support, compassion, understanding, and help in our times of need. He is a gracious God who draws near to us in our hardest moments, and He'd rather we process our grief or frustration in *His* presence as opposed to stuffing them down and ignoring them.

However, what I am saying is that though there's a place to mourn the constant sacrifices required to live this military life, there's also a place to be thankful for them at the same time. They are the very circumstances by which the Holy Spirit works in us, maturing us and helping us to look more and more like Christ—the One whose most terrible life circumstance (the cross) ended up being used for good.

Purpose Three: Service

As military wives, it feels like we serve and serve and serve our husbands. It's all too easy to think we shouldn't have to love him extravagantly and sacrificially when we're exhausted because *we just followed him across the country again* (or whatever else the sacrifice)!

However, our service toward our spouse is not conditional. Jesus modeled the necessity of lovingly and sacrificially serving those around us. He didn't do it for thanks, applause, self-worth, or to increase His tally of good acts. He did it because He loved God and wanted to honor His Father, not because he was subservient. So, when we serve our spouses, it's helpful to remember that we're ultimately worshipping God by how we love our husbands.

Even if your husband's heart isn't inclined to serve you the same way, you're still maturing in your faith and pointing your spouse to Jesus as you use the opportunity to grow into the likeness of Christ. When I focus on the Lord instead of my marital scoreboard, the Holy Spirit gives me the capability to serve Tim with an open heart, leaving the tally-marking pen on the table. It no longer becomes about Tim acknowledging the good I'm doing because I know *God* feels honored with my work—whether that's faithfully changing a dirty diaper, cleaning the bathrooms, leading a homeschool lesson, writing an article, raking the leaves, or taking out the trash.

However, my fallen nature continues to fail me because I occasionally bring out that old tally pen. Hopefully, I'll use it less and less the more and more I focus on God. (As an aside, trying not to keep score doesn't mean you can't respectfully communicate your hurts to your spouse when appropriate. Open and honest communication is yet another way to serve your marriage!)

Modeling Jesus: Love Your Neighbor

During Jesus's life, two groups of Jewish religious leaders wanted Jesus dead with vehement passion, the Pharisees and the Sadducees. They lived their entire lives to uphold God's rules, but tragically, they missed the whole point. The Hope of the world stood right before them, yet their hardened hearts couldn't soften to the Savior. Instead, beliefs and desires blinded them.

One day, the Pharisees intentionally tried to trap Jesus into saying something to negate God's law. They needed to create a reason to accuse Jesus before the Roman government, validating their request for His execution. A pharisaic lawyer asked Jesus which of God's commandments was the greatest. Jesus responded by saying:

> "Love the Lord your God with all your heart, with all your soul, and with all your mind. This is the greatest and most important command. The second is like it: Love your neighbor as yourself. All the Law and the Prophets depend on these two commands." (Matt. 22:37–40)

The Greek word Jesus uses for "love" is *agapaó*, which means "to love, wish well to, take pleasure in, long for; denotes the love of reason, esteem."[4] Nine times across Scripture, God tells us to love our neighbor using *agapaó*-type love. And who is your most intimate neighbor? Right—your spouse. Jesus also tells us to love our neighbor as we love *ourselves*. Most of us reflexively care for our own physical and emotional needs; we eat when we're hungry, rest when we're tired, cry when we are overwhelmed, and so on. God wants us to love our spouses similarly, paying attention to their needs.

If we're to live the way God wants us to and thus experience true freedom and joy (despite the unavoidable agitations and trials of life), we can't fall victim to the enemy's trap that aims to harden our hearts due to "what's right" and "what should be." There were no stipulations to this command to love God and your neighbor. Jesus didn't say love your neighbor unless he misses dinner most nights, or his orders make you move again, or his commander calls him back out to training, or he falls asleep without helping, and so on. There may be times you're correct about the way things should be, but this "rightness" doesn't negate Jesus's call to love. Imagine if Jesus only loved us and served us when we were acting according to the way things should be!

If you want to experience the most purposeful, intentional, rewarding marriage, it comes down to loving God and loving your closest neighbor—the person you married. Living life the way Jesus lived is essential to our peace and joy. But, if we try to do it our way, we'll miss it every time, making the same tragic mistake as the Pharisees.

———————————— *Prayer* ————————————

Dear God,

Thank You for the gift of marriage, which You designed with expert craftsmanship I cannot begin to appreciate or grasp. Through this beautifully complex relationship, You've created the opportunity for me to love and serve a broken person. And You've given me the gift of being loved and served in return, despite my brokenness. But God, when I don't feel loved by my husband, give me the ability through the Holy Spirit to continue loving him in return, knowing that I am glorifying You and maturing in my faith. Remind me, Lord, that only You can truly fulfill me. Help me release the unreasonable expectation for my husband to be everything to me and meet all my needs. And God, protect my marriage from the enemy, who desperately aims to destroy it. Give my husband and me the discernment to recognize Satan's interferences and not blame them on each other. In all this, please help me to see my military marriage as Your blessing and conduit of spiritual growth, not a burden. Show me how to honor You with this gift, Lord. In Jesus's loving name, amen.

Reflection Questions

1. Growing up, did anyone in your life teach you about the foundations of biblical marriage?

2. What did you think the ultimate purpose of your marriage was when you got married?

3. How does understanding God's design for marriage change your perspective on your role as a wife?

4. What challenges about military life can you view as a blessing because they're shaping your character and allowing you the opportunity to look more like Jesus?

5. In what area of your marriage can you serve your husband with Christlike love (*not* because you're subservient to him but because you aim to model the love of Christ in your marriage)?

Next Steps

- ❑ Read the Scriptures every day.
- ❑ Create friendships with women who value marriage.
- ❑ Designate time in your daily schedule to prioritize your marriage.

❏ Join a community that intentionally seeks to develop godly marriage skills.

❏ Pray specific and strategic prayers daily for your husband.

❏ Make an appointment to receive Christian marriage counseling together or individually.

❏ Find and regularly attend a church that believes in God's design for marriage.

❏ Ask a woman whose godly marriage you admire to mentor you.

❏ Seek immediate help if you are in an abusive marriage.

Resources

For links and descriptions of each resource, visit Ashleyashcraft.com/missionreadymarriage.

- *Sacred Marriage* by Gary Thomas
- *The Meaning of Marriage* by Timothy Keller
- *This Momentary Marriage* by John Piper
- *Kingdom Marriage* by Tony Evans
- *The Gift of Sex* by Clifford and Joyce Penner
- *What Did You Expect?* by Paul David Tripp
- *Fight for Us* by Chad M. Robichaux and Adam Davis
- *Fierce Marriage* podcast
- *The Naked Marriage* podcast
- *Delight Your Marriage* podcast

Chapter Three

Duty: An Alignment of Assignments

Do you think you play a *significant* role in
the armed forces as a military spouse?
Circle One: Yes / No

Did you feel like you married into a secret society with a foreign language the day you became a military spouse? Or was it all familiar because your parents served in the armed services while you grew up? We come to this military lifestyle with an immeasurable variance of understanding and personal background, yet we each hold this book because we fell in love with someone who pledged an oath to uphold the Constitution.

That commonality creates an unspoken bond between you, me, and everyone else who said "I do" to a service member. Our lives are sewn together within the fabric of the American flag–enlisted, officer, guard, and reserve alike. Our husbands chose to offer their lives as a commitment to what those Stars and Stripes uphold; we did the same when we pledged our marriage vows, whether we knew it or not.

A Service Member's Assignment

Have you ever heard the oath your husband swore to the United States when he joined the military? Some of us were present that day, watching in a military office, an aircraft hangar, a museum, or beneath a historical statue. Others of us had not yet met our spouse on the day he repeated the words read off by a military officer.

Tim pledged his oath to the military on a muggy Hudson Valley afternoon on May 26, 2007. An hour before, I watched in awe as he shook Vice President Cheney's hand and accepted his diploma from West Point. The pomp and circumstance of a West Point graduation felt like I'd snuck into some royal modern-day knighting ceremony.

Tim quickly changed into his never-before-worn greens and stood under the awning of an old brick building on West Point. He raised his right hand and took the oath of office that would sculpt the rest of our lives. They are the exact words your husband repeated as well. Here are the words (for both officers and enlisted) that direct everything our husbands do in their profession as a service member:

Oath of Commissioned Officers

I, _____, do solemnly swear (or affirm) that I will support and defend the Constitution of the United States against all enemies, foreign and domestic; that I will bear true faith and allegiance to the same; that I take this obligation freely, without any mental reservation or purpose of evasion; and that I will well and faithfully discharge the duties of the office upon which I am about to enter. So help me God.

Oath of Enlistment

I, _____, do solemnly swear (or affirm) that I will support and defend the Constitution of the United States against all enemies, foreign and domestic; that I will bear true faith and allegiance to the same; and that I will obey the orders of the President of the United States and the orders of the officers appointed over me, according to regulations and the Uniform Code of Military Justice. So help me God.

Ultimately, our husbands' jobs revolve around always being ready to deploy. The necessity of deployment readiness is the reason for the sheer craziness we live through as spouses—the long work hours, frequent absences, incessant moving, solo parenting, and full responsibility for all things on the home front (to name a few!).

Being a military spouse is desperately challenging because our husbands must train unceasingly to survive. Period. A military leader's job is to prepare each service member for war, and even though they cannot guarantee everyone returns alive, that leader must train his troops to a measure that seems excessive to us. We want our husbands to show up around the dinner table, and even though it feels like their leaders are taking them away from us, those same leaders are actually trying to make sure they can give our husbands back to us when they've fulfilled their commitment to our country.

My husband recently listened to a commanding general who recalled a story of a Gold Star mother who approached him after losing her son. (A Gold Star Family is the family of a fallen service member who died in the line of duty.) She asked the general if he had done everything possible to prepare her son for war. He answered, "Yes."

In the mundane repetitions of married life, we cannot forget the weight and seriousness—literally life and death—of our husband's responsibilities as a service member. Some of them are leaders equipping their fellow unit members for combat. Others are essential personnel fulfilling indispensable orders, while still others offer vital support to the mission. So whether your husband is a pilot, paratrooper, special operator, refueler, intel personnel, engineer, teacher, cyber specialist, doctor, lawyer, chaplain, transporter, or any other MOS (military occupational specialty), his assignment is crucial.

I like the way my husband sums up a service member's assignment for us:

> Everything is predicated on readiness to deploy; therefore, hard and certain frequencies of training have to be maintained. The longer you're in, the more responsibility you have—not just for your own readiness but for the readiness of others.

Honestly, when I think about my husband's job this way, it's easier for me to maintain a healthy level of self-control in the natural frustrations that come with the sacrifices of being a military spouse. When I think only about myself and my kids, it's easy for anger to escalate when the military has seemingly no regard for my family. However, training my brain to remember the weight of my husband's job and his responsibility to make sure his Soldiers make it home safely from combat helps temper my frustrations. *Those Soldiers have their own families and homes and dinner tables,* I tell myself often, *and to get home in one piece, they desperately need the training my husband provides.*

A Military Spouse's Assignment

I almost wish that as I stood under the hundred-year-old stained-glass windows in a laced cream wedding gown, a military chaplain would have joined us on the altar to administer *my* military spouse oath. (No such oath exists, but what if it did?) Before the pastor sent us down the aisle as husband and wife, I envision the chaplain asking me to repeat the following words after him, my right hand raised:

> I, Ashley Ashcraft, do solemnly affirm that I will support my husband in his defense of the Constitution of the United States; that I will bear true faith and allegiance to the same; that I take this obligation freely, without any mental reservation or purpose of evasion; and that I will well and faithfully discharge the duties of the role in which I am about to enter. So help me God.

In my imagined scenario, the chaplain would then welcome me into the fold of the flag, recognizing my role in defense of our nation's Stars and Stripes. Even though pledging that oath wouldn't practically equip me for a military marriage, I feel like it would have cemented a necessary foundation for the depth of commitment required for one.

Truth be told, I don't need the military to offer me the opportunity to say this oath, nor do you. Ultimately, we agree to it when we say "I do," but our families can be healthier the more clarity we uncover in our roles as military wives. You know, that whole expectation management thing.

Now, no official military document defines our roles as military spouses, yet our support to the health of our service member and his unit is invaluable. Over the last fifteen years, I've watched women do this with intentionality, and I've witnessed many others give up. Below is a list of ways to selflessly serve your husband and the military, modeled to me by many inspiring military spouses. These wives decided to overcome the challenges of the armed services with a mission-minded mentality.

- Participate in unit events to build relationships and support unit intent.
- Care for your family in the absence of your service member.
- Create a village to support you wherever you live. (Don't wait for it to find you.)
- Support other military spouses and their children.
- Honor your husband's mission and sacrifice to the nation.
- Respect your husband as he fulfills his duty to country.
- Daily depend on God.
- Invest your time in the Scriptures.
- Trust God in the perpetual trials.
- Notice areas of unmet need in the unit and partner with others to fulfill that need.
- Mentor and befriend younger military spouses.

So, how do we take our husband's assignment as a service member and our assignment as a military spouse and create an atmosphere of cohesion and partnership?

What's My Purpose Here, God?

When our husbands get assignments to new duty stations, it's easy to feel like a dispensable cardboard box on the moving truck, packed and loaded like all the other contents of your house. (Just me?) Sometimes I even want to be that cardboard box that mysteriously disappears on the way to the next installation. The military wouldn't even notice; the mission would continue without me. But that's a lie. I *am* needed at the next duty station, equally as much as my Soldier.

Everything went wrong during our ninth move, from Alabama to New York. The kids came down with a fever, we didn't get everything packed on time, and the hitch on the SUV we purchased to tow our other car (so we could drive together as a family) broke.

So I drove behind my husband's navy blue Ford Explorer with a teething, feverish child screaming in discomfort, my life in boxes on some truck in an unknown location, and no home, friends, or family waiting when we got to the mountains of New York. It was all too easy to wonder why I was doing this, again, for the *ninth* time! What was in it for me? Why did I have to keep moving my life around the globe because the Army told my husband to PCS (permanent change of station)? By the way, can we all agree that the word *permanent* is quite ridiculous in this acronym?

I searched relentlessly for "my purpose" at each new station for the first decade of my husband's service. Often the doors shut on what I thought I was supposed to do, or I couldn't figure it out. *Why aren't You using me here, God? What do You want me to do? I'm lost!*

Women notoriously struggle with this idea of purpose: identifying and executing it. As a result, we can become stressed and stagnant in this cycle of searching and waiting for God to reveal this great mystery. Throw in the military's stopwatch counting down our hours before we even arrive at each base, and a military spouse may feel a dire urgency to discover her new purpose at every location. We only get, on average, one to three years before we have to move on and figure it out all over again.

But here's the good news: you don't have to search any longer for your purpose because God reveals it in the Scriptures. Your context may change each time you move, but your purpose (your assignment) does not. In Matthew 28:18–20 Jesus declares,

> "All authority has been given to me in heaven
> and on earth. *Go*, therefore, and *make* disciples
> of all nations, *baptizing* them in the name of
> the Father and of the Son and of the Holy Spirit,
> *teaching* them to observe everything I have
> commanded you. And remember, I am with you
> always, to the end of the age." (emphasis added)

Boom. That's it; you don't have to wonder anymore. There's your assignment: go, make, baptize, and teach. And that's your husband's mission too. Everywhere God sends you and your family, He commands you to live out Matthew 28:18–20. In fact, this Bible passage is known as the Great Commission. If you are a follower of Christ, *this* is your purpose.

So, when God uses the military to move you and your husband, He's enabling you to *go* to a new place so you can partner with him to *make* disciples there (other followers of Jesus). Friend, God has people He wants to rescue in that new location, bringing them to saving knowledge of His Son. And to make sure a messenger of the gospel gets to those people, He's intentionally sending *you*! So when you get there, remember He wants you to help others seek Him as you share the good news with them. And when these people become believers, He wants you to encourage them to get *baptized* at a nearby church (baptism is an outward, public profession of their new, inward faith). After becoming a believer and getting baptized, they need to grow, which is why this passage tells you to *teach* them to obey God. And how do you teach a person to obey God? Study God's Word with them, pray with them, go to church with them, and use your own life as an example to them—the kind of example you always wanted when you were first growing in Christ. *Go, make, baptize, teach.* That's the assignment.

I also appreciate the simplicity of how John Piper describes our purpose in his book *Desiring God*. Piper explains that we were created to "be happy in God, to delight in God, to cherish and enjoy His fellowship and favor."[1] That's it. Why do we make the idea of purpose so complicated? When we enjoy and exalt our heavenly Father, we naturally seek ways to actively love others and share the gospel because of our deep love for Him.

Alignment of Assignment

Because God placed you and your husband together, He interlocked your assignments. Your service to the military as a *couple* is a team effort to support the nation and spread the gospel (the good news of Jesus). If God assigned your husband work to do at Fort Bliss, you also have work to do at Fort Bliss. There are people He needs you to create relationships with, churches He needs you to serve in, units He needs you to support, and communities in which He needs you to invest.

Also, we find ourselves in a slightly different season each time we move. So it's helpful to consider your current state before you invest. You may be newly married at one base, pregnant and caring for babies at another, living with toddlers and preschoolers at the next, or finding more free time with school-aged children. You might be geographically separated from your spouse if circumstances require you to stay back while he moved. You might be dealing with deployment or reintegration. Or you may be entering into the preparation for completing your enlistment period or retiring after twenty to thirty years of service.

It's all too easy (and familiar for me!) to focus on myself and the sacrifice I'm already making simply by being a military spouse. Why shouldn't I stay in my chaotic little world and merely survive the latest move until we have to pack up again? Unfortunately, I can't serve others in that state of mind because I'm worried about myself. However, Jesus calls us to look outside ourselves and help others as we pursue a life that desires to follow Him.

And that's where everything falls into place for me, and the craziness of this military life starts to make sense. Serving those around you looks different for all of us, and it changes with each season. So here are some ideas to help you step into a life of service in the military that honors the assignment God has given us to go and make disciples:

- Volunteer at your installation's food pantry for enlisted service members and families.
- Collect donations for service families in need during the holidays.
- Host a Bible study for your unit or in your neighborhood.
- Help your unit's family support program (or volunteer to be the leader)!
- Ask your local church about opportunities to serve.
- Join the Giving Tuesday Military Community Online.
- Help out at the local Veterans of Foreign Wars chapter.
- Volunteer at your children's school.

In all of these examples, you actually serve in two ways at once. You meet a direct need (feeding the hungry, completing tasks the school needs accomplished, etc.), but you also begin the process of developing relationships that help you *go, make, baptize,* and *teach.* In each of these arenas, there are people who have never heard of Jesus, and as you serve shoulder to shoulder with them, a friendship may blossom—one that could eventually result in their coming to Christ and learning to follow Him. All because you embraced the Great Commission assignment!

A Word on Saying No

As I've stated, there is a coming and passing of seasons in our lives. So you may not always be able to serve in the military community due to life circumstances. And that's okay, perfectly okay.

At our first duty station, my husband's company commander was single, which meant there was no natural Family Readiness Group (now called the Soldier FRG, or SFRG) leader. So when Tim stepped in as a married platoon leader, the commander asked if I would lead the company's FRG. At that time, I could serve my husband's unit and accepted the position, although I didn't have a clue what I was signing up for. Thankfully, the military loves training, so I was well informed after several classes.

However, eleven years later, we entered another unit without an SFRG leader. When Tim showed up as the new executive officer, one of the first questions was whether his wife would lead the FRG. I immediately said no without shame or hesitation.

During that time in my life, I was about to start homeschooling for the first time, my children were dealing with a host of medical issues, I recently signed a contract to be a contributing writer for a publishing project, and, oh yeah, we had just moved for the twelfth time. I acknowledged that adding that responsibility to my life would be more than I could handle.

I served and loved where I could, attending unit events, hosting an occasional spouse event, engaging with unit spouses on social media, and regularly babysitting for a woman because her husband had deployed to the Middle East. Those areas of service required sacrifice, but they were ones I could manage without my life crumbling from the weight of stress and exhaustion.

So, if you're moving while pregnant, loving on a newborn, wrangling toddlers, living with a chronic illness, or dealing with some other limiting challenge, feel free to say no to hands-on service when you need to. However, just because you can't physically serve doesn't mean you won't have an impact where God's placed you.

One significant way you can invest your time from home is through prayer. In Romans 12, Paul gives a list of ways Christians should live. In verse 12, he says, "Rejoice in hope; be patient in affliction; be persistent in prayer." Pray for the unit's members, the leaders, and the families. Pray for God to use others as the hands and feet of Jesus, sharing the hope of Christ within the unit.

Finally, you don't need to serve a crowd to fulfill the Great Commission. In certain seasons when leaving home is hard, God may want you to dedicate your time to the military community right in front of you—your children and your husband. Teaching and loving your family are worthy and eternal endeavors. The goal, ultimately, is to be *honest* about what you can and cannot do and offer whatever you can do to the Lord, asking Him to multiply your investment and bring others to know Him. Being honest means not hiding behind excuses when you know God is calling you to start serving in some way, and it also means not saying yes when you know God is calling you to take a step back!

Modeling Jesus: Sacrifice in Marriage

Many people who are not followers of Jesus do good in this world. You don't have to believe in Him to help others; however, we're here to align our place in the military with the mission of the kingdom of God. Therefore, the reason you are a military spouse matters. You didn't arbitrarily marry a service member. Instead, God placed you both here for His purpose, to partner with God in ushering others into a relationship with the King of kings.

This alignment of God's assignment between a service member and spouse requires sacrifice: the sacrifice of time, place, comfort, resources, and energy. Are you willing to give those items to God to use them as He wills?

The truth is, you already have to give up this stuff with or without God. The military moves you to places you don't always want to go, certainly at inconvenient times. You regularly lose any established comforts of location and people. Moving costs and military expenses continually drain your resources. And the energy it takes to constantly move and reestablish your life (housing, primary medical care, dentistry, specialists, Internet, electrical, gas, water, trash, schools, jobs, friendships, church, libraries, etc.) is a buried treasure I've never been able to locate. As a result, I'm running on fumes most days.

Yet, if I *choose* to partner with God on this "adventure," there's a purpose for all the sacrifices. It's not all ruck and suck. There are intentional sacrifices I can make to honor God within the boundaries He's defined for me in the military. But I get to choose if I'll make them with a hardened heart or a soft one surrendered to God's will.

In the hours before Jesus was taken prisoner on the Mount of Olives, knowing the brutal infliction of trauma about to accost his earthly body, He prayed for God to change the story. In Luke 22:42, Jesus says, "Father, if you are willing, take this cup away from me—nevertheless, not my will, but yours, be done." Jesus's concession following his request is imperative here! When we want God to change our story—the newly cut PCS orders, the impending deployment, or the battle wound—we must follow our request with these sacrificial words: nevertheless, not my will, but Yours, be done.

God's ways are higher than our own. We cannot begin to fathom the depths of the plans He creates. So when Christ sacrificially offered His body per the will of His Father, He trusted God's goodness even as He agonized over the torturous fate that awaited Him on the intersection of two trees. We, too, have a choice to make. When we want our circumstances to change, will we submit to and obey God's will or charge forward on a different path?

Because God loves us, He gave us free will. And let me tell you, my free will is strong! It's got an opinion it wants to fight for and defend. But as my faith in Christ deepens, I'm choosing to restrain my wild free will more and more. We can do this challenging military life with God or without. Will you join me in choosing Him? Will you allow Him to use your sacrifices for the glory of the kingdom? Will you accept this assignment and witness what God can do through one military wife who has given her full yes to *go, make, baptize,* and *teach*?

Prayer

Dear Heavenly Father,

Thank You for loving me and choosing a unique path for me based on Your incomprehensible wisdom. Help me honor and glorify You, no matter where You assign us to live. Show me how to submit my ways to You for your purposes. Lord, help me fulfill the Great

Commission, to go and make disciples within the military community you've placed me in. God, help me align my assignment to the one You've given my husband. Show us how to partner with You on mission for Your kingdom. In Jesus's sacrificial name, amen.

Reflection Questions

1. Did you understand the scope of your commitment when you married a service member?

2. What information do you wish faith leaders, seasoned spouses, or someone from your husband's unit would have shared with you to help you prepare for life as a military wife?

3. From the lists of ways to selflessly serve your husband, the military, and community (listed on pages 34 and 39), which one would be the easiest for you to implement, and which one seems the most daunting? Why?

4. How would you have defined your purpose within the military community before reading this chapter? Now that you've explored the Great Commission that Jesus gives us, in what ways has your previous purpose changed?

5. What is the most significant thing God is asking you to sacrifice to partner with Him as a follower of Christ in the military community? Are you willing to submit to His will for you, even when it requires sacrifice?

6. As you consider implementing the four phases of the Great Commission—go, make, baptize, and teach—which of the four is a strength for you? Which feels like a weakness? How could you grow in the area you feel weak?

Next Steps

❑ Identify your gifts and talents to know how
to serve (see resources below to guide you).

❑ Ask your unit chaplain how you can help.

❑ Find opportunities for how you can serve in
your local church.

❑ Ask your husband how you can best support
him in his assignment.

❑ Share with your husband how he can best
support *you* in *your* assignment as a military
spouse.

Resources

For links and descriptions of each resource, visit
Ashleyashcraft.com/missionreadymarriage.

- *Wife of a Soldier* by Diana Juergens
- *Fly Safe* by Vicki Cody
- *Master Plan of Evangelism* by Robert Coleman
- *Sharing Jesus without Freaking Out* by Scott
Hildreth and Steven McKinion
- *Milspouse Matters* podcast
- *Military OneSource* podcast
- S.H.A.P.E. Test
- Cru's Spiritual Gifts Quiz
- Cru Military's Resource Store
- *Military Spouse* magazine
- *Military Families* magazine

- Blue Star Families
- Association of Military Spouse Entrepreneurs
- National Military Family Association
- My Career Advancement Account
- MilSpo Project
- Military Spouse Advocacy Network
- The Rosie Network
- Instant Teams

Chapter Four

Faith: Creating Hope and Health in Spiritual Disciplines

The biggest hinderance I have with my
faith is _____.

Every night after I tuck my kids in bed, my footsteps quicken down our wooden staircase so I can quietly soak in too-hot water that relaxes my mind and body. I turn the silver handle and as the water rushes urgently out, I pour in lavender Epsom salts or aloe vera bubbles. As I step into my little oasis, I'm tempted to open a video streaming or social media app and mindlessly watch or scroll after spending the last thirteen hours with my *extraordinarily spirited* children. However, I've noticed that's not a healthy regular practice for me.

Instead, I've disciplined myself to spend this time reading. I don't always want to do it (and sometimes I don't), but for the most part, I consistently turn pages while my skin prunes in water that turns cool before I want to stop. Since I was a little frizzy-haired girl, I've recognized the benefits of reading are worth my investment of time.

This is also true of spiritual disciplines: we don't always want to do them, but they're worth our investment. By "disciplines" I simply mean practices, or things we do. We don't always want to do them, but we know they're good for us. They grow us, mature us, make us stronger, and wiser.

The basic spiritual practices described in this chapter help us lean into God in the face of the perpetual trials we face as military spouses. Honestly, if not for the saving grace of Jesus, I don't know how I'd find joy in a military marriage, let alone survive it.

A couple of years in, there was a moment when I thought about packing my bags and heading back to the desert I call home. Military marriage was hard (an understatement of the century!), and doing it on my own wasn't working. I needed God's guidance to transcend the inevitable challenges.

A Pre-Wedding Chat with God

Often, I like to picture God sitting next to me as I talk to Him or walking with me while I pray. It helps my brain fathom the reality that He *really is* with me and hearing me even though I can't see Him. I visualize His expression, His posture, and His clothes. Today, I had a moment when I wondered what God may have said to me at the very beginning of this journey in the military. I pictured Him lovingly holding my hand, a Father speaking His last words of wisdom before His daughter takes on the role of wife. Here's what I thought He might say to me—and you.

Dear _____ (fill in your name),

I've chosen for you to marry a military man. It's going to be hard. But I will be with you every step of the way. Every move. Every disappointment. Every blessing. Every new job and new child. Every new church and place you serve. Every deployment and training that separates you and your husband. You're going to be scared at times, my dear.

You'll get phone calls that leave you in fear, and you'll have to trust Me when you don't know what's coming. You'll watch your friends lose their husbands to bullets, crashes, and PTSD. I need you to try your best to love those who become widows and orphans. You won't know how to do it in the beginning. But you'll learn. And when it happens again, show up.

I chose to place you in this community for this time. I don't want you to do it alone, though. I'll put people in your life at each post to encourage and support you, even if it's just one or two. Please learn from them and practice the wisdom they offer. And remember, I gave you the Holy Spirit to guide you. Listen to Him.

And when it's time to move, remember that I'm the One in charge. I'm using the military to take you to where I need you. There are people there I need you to connect with that you would not encounter otherwise. I know it would be easier to stay, but you know I'm not after easy. I told you following Me would be hard and uncomfortable. But if you trust Me, you'll see it's worth it.

And most importantly, _____, make the time to get to know Me more every day. Open the Scriptures, and let Me share with you. Allow Me to teach, refine, and love you through My Word. It's the only thing that will hold you together when you feel like you can't do it anymore, and it's what you'll need to equip you where I'm taking you.

And when you realize you're trying to do this alone, stop. Ask for help. I know that might feel scary, but you need to reach out. I didn't plan for you to live in isolation; that's a tactic of the enemy. Instead, I want you to live in community, to thrive among brothers and sisters in Christ. So if you move and can't find one, you must create one. Remember, I am a God of creation, and you are My image bearer. You, too, are made to create.

Above all, remember that I love you—more than you can comprehend. I am for you, child. Everything that happens will eventually work out for your good, even when you don't understand. I promise. I will never leave you.

*Now, let's get you married. We have important
things to accomplish.*

I love you,

God

So, how do we purposely live out this Great Commission,
our God-given assignment? It starts with faith in Jesus Christ,
and we live that out with the help of spiritual disciplines or
practices. I love this dynamic statement from Craig Dykstra to
get us started: "Practices are the nuclear reactors of the Christian
faith, arenas where the gospel and human life come together in
energizing, even explosive ways. Practices create openings in our
lives where the grace, mercy, and presence of God may be made
known to us."[1]

To aid us in walking out our faith as military spouses, let's
look at a few spiritual disciplines that can help us experience and
share the hope of Jesus.

Get Involved in Your Local Church

They devoted themselves to the apostles'
teaching, to the fellowship, to the breaking of
bread, and to prayer. (Acts 2:42)

As a new believer at twenty-three, I remember standing awk-
wardly in the back of a white-steepled church, afraid to stand by
myself while my husband played onstage in the worship band. I
stood stiffly and breathed shallowly, fearing what others thought
of my presence there.

Over time, my faithful attendance became comfortable. I looked forward to Sundays with eager anticipation. Now, I'm in the front row crying tears of gratitude, singing horribly off pitch, and lifting my arms in praise. I can't help it! Coming together with the body of Christ is the highlight of my week.

We established an essential rhythm in our marriage at our first military installation—finding a church, no excuses. My husband and I have prioritized this in our family, no matter where the military sends us. When orders arrive, we start researching churches near our new installation. Sometimes we get a church recommendation from someone who has previously been stationed where we're headed. Other times, we do a simple Internet search for churches in our new area. We check out their website and listen to sermons posted there.

It's like dating: you might have to try a few before finding the right fit. However, you won't find a perfect church, because they're all run by imperfect people. So instead, pick one that believes the Bible is the inspired Word of God, unashamedly teaches what it says, loves its people, and serves joyfully.

We've had to try several churches at some posts before finding one we both liked. Sometimes we had to drive thirty minutes to get to church. And every week, without fail, there's a kid protesting attendance. And always, we're late (sorry, Babe). But we go. And it's always worth it.

Hebrews 10:24–25 shows us God's plan for us to meet together as believers:

> And let us consider one another in order to
> provoke love and good works, not neglecting
> to gather together, as some are in the habit of

doing, but encouraging each other, and all the
more as you see the day approaching.

When we fail to meet together, we go against God's plan
to live in a community with other believers. But, unfortunately,
there's a growing trend of isolation within the military spouse
community that we have to fight against proactively. We have to
pick up and put down our lives so often that the idea of building
relationships with others in the church seems too exhausting to
manage. But God designed us for this connection that encourages us and leads us toward love and good works.

We also need a group of trusted people we can rely on when
our husband is deployed or off training and the kids get sick, or
the car breaks down. The church is a beautiful and safe place to
connect with people who can care for us spiritually, emotionally,
and physically, especially in our husband's absence.

However, God doesn't call us just to attend church. We also
need to offer the church the gifts God blessed us with to benefit
others. In 1 Corinthians 12, Paul explains how God designed
each believer to serve as part of one body. Verse 27 says, "You
are the body of Christ, and each one of you is a part of it" (NIV).

When looking for volunteers, one of our former churches
reported that only 10 percent of those attending serve in the
church. So let's engage that part of the body we represent and
help the church. Ask your church volunteer coordinator where
you can help. Let them know the areas where you enjoy serving
and inform them of your gifts. Remember, you need the gifts
other people offer, and they need yours! Think of it this way: who
gets robbed of the thing they need most when you don't show up
to share your spiritual gift with them (perhaps yours is prayer,

mercy, faith, hospitality, encouragement, teaching, or otherwise)? And what ministry do *you* need from others that you're being robbed of if you don't show up to receive it? Don't hoard your gift at home when your gift could benefit someone else, and don't cheat yourself of the benefits you need in this season that could come from the ministry of another church member. The only way church works is if all members show up to share their gifts and resources with others.

Now, here's the truth: people run churches, and people are sinful. Maybe you've been hurt by a church before, or the pastor preached false teaching. Perhaps the worship music was too loud, or the kids didn't like their class. Maybe the chaplain taught a little too long, or they didn't offer coffee and doughnuts. Whatever human issues and frustrations exist, mourn them and process them. But at the same time, don't let them stand in the way of honoring God within the community of your fellow brothers and sisters in Christ. Choose a healthy church with good teaching and kind shepherds. It won't be perfect, but it's worth it.

Reading the Scriptures

> For whatever was written in the past was
> written for our instruction, so that we may
> have hope through endurance and through
> the encouragement from the Scriptures.
> (Rom. 15:4)

Right here is where it's at, my friend—reading God's Word. There's nothing else in the world remotely like it. It's the best-selling book of *all time* for a reason. This book is so unexplainably special that in countries where the text is forbidden, believers knowingly risk imprisonment, torture, and death to be able to read God's unchanging, life-giving Word.

A health-related study of military spouses titled "Everything Else Comes First"[2] concluded that military spouses deal with unique stressors that impede them from prioritizing their health. The stressors listed included "frequent moves, isolation from family and friends, unpredictable changes, and uncertainty about the well-being of the spouse during combat operations." In addition, the study looked at physical activity, social connection, stress management, and diet.

All this leaves us at an increased risk for poor physical and mental health, especially obesity, depression, and anxiety. The study goes on to state, "A review of the literature on military spouse health shows research has primarily demonstrated negative effects of the military lifestyle on spouses' mental health and the marital relationship." Probably not shocking news to you.

Any of you holding this book could have told me the above conclusion. However, did you notice what was missing from this study on military spouse health? That's right, spiritual health. Our spiritual health is *essential* to completing the military spouse health overview. And the military spouse community is spiritually *starving*!

However, another study of forty thousand Americans conducted by the Center of Bible Engagement (CBE) offers great hope. But first, let's look at the problem they discovered. The study found that 71 percent of eighteen- to twenty-four-year-olds and 68 percent of those twenty-five and older never read the Bible, and the number is only a couple of percentages lower for those who identify as born-again Christians.

They discovered that people who read the Bible *four or more* times per week engaged significantly less in risky behaviors, like getting drunk, 57 percent lower odds; sex outside marriage, 68 percent lower odds; pornography, 61 percent lower odds; and gambling, 74 percent lower odds. Of note, those reading the Bible *one to three times per week* showed *no lower odds*. So, if reading God's Word does this for the above negative behaviors, what do you think it could do for the stress, depression, and anxiety many of us regularly face?

As discussed in chapter 2, our assignment in the military community is to share the gospel. This study by the CBE shows a dramatic increase in effectiveness in a person reading the Scriptures four or more times per week. Look at this:

> More Scripture engagement also produces a Christian who is more involved in spreading the Good News. Controlling for other factors, those who read or listen to the Bible at least four days a week have higher odds of participating in these behaviors: sharing faith with others = 228% higher odds; discipling others = 231% higher odds, and memorizing scripture = 407% higher odds.[3]

Why is no one talking about this? The answer to a lot of our issues is right here! And it's probably sitting on your bookshelf at home. Will you join me in making this a regular daily discipline?

Practically speaking, fitting *another* task into your life is hard. I get it. Your mornings are full, your afternoons are busy, bedtime with kids is chaotic (let's be honest!), and by the time the day is over, you're too exhausted to even think about reading God's Word. However, where we spend our time and money reflects our priorities. Where is God on that list?

Starting a daily reading practice is going to take commitment. Start by challenging yourself to sixty-three days of reading the Scriptures to help you develop this new habit. Dr. Caroline Leaf, a neuroscientist who specializes in cognitive and metacognitive neuropsychology, states,

> Trying to change yourself too fast can cause unnecessary stress, making you more anxious and setting you up for what I call the "shame spiral" . . . because you feel like you keep failing and are not able to change. But it takes a minimum of 63 days to change an automated habit—when it comes to the mind, there really are no quick fixes and most people give up on day 4, so be patient![4]

At first, it may feel like a task, but in time, meeting with God in His Word becomes a sanctuary you can't wait to step inside.

Choose a rhythm that works for your life, understanding that it will fluctuate as life changes. As a woman with young kids who require constant attention, I must fight for my time in the Word. Currently, I read the Bible after breakfast while my kids play. When I was a new mom, I read while nursing my babies. When my kids were toddlers, I woke up early to read. Some moms listen to an audio version of the Bible while doing chores, working out, or driving to work. Others prefer to listen to the Bible while they do their nighttime routine or read it right before bed as a way to calm down from the day and remember the promises of God. Figure out where you can carve out time and make it happen. The time is there, I promise.

Sharing the Gospel

And he said to them, "Go into all the world
and proclaim the gospel to the whole creation."
(Mark 16:15 ESV)

Sharing the gospel feels intimidating to many Christians. *What if I mess it up? What if I say the wrong thing? What if it doesn't make sense?* I listened to former Army Ranger and chaplain Jeff Strueker talk about how a young married couple shared the gospel with him as a teenager. He explained how nervous they were and how they "stumbled all over themselves." But he went on to explain that "it all made sense." That couple's lack of eloquence didn't stand in Jeff's way of accepting the gospel, and their faithfulness in sharing the hope of Jesus with Jeff honored God in more ways than they'll probably ever know! As I think about that faithful couple's choice to share the gospel, even if it meant fumbling their way through it, I'm reminded of the apostle Paul's words in 1 Corinthians 2:1–5 (NIV): "When I came to you, I did not come with eloquence or human wisdom as I proclaimed to you the testimony about God. For I resolved to know nothing while I was with you except Jesus Christ and him crucified. I came to you in weakness with great fear and trembling. My message and my preaching were not with wise and persuasive words, but with a demonstration of the Spirit's power, so that your faith might not rest on human wisdom, but on God's power." May we all adopt this posture![5]

When sharing the gospel, it's essential to recognize that you are not responsible for anyone's salvation—that's God's job alone. He commands us to go and tell, but He is the One who opens hearts and minds to believe in Him. The most important information to communicate is that Jesus Christ switched places with us in order to erase our sin and restore our relationship with the Father, enabling us to live with Him for eternity in heaven. In His earthly ministry, Jesus lived the life we should have lived—in our place. On the cross, He died the death for wrongdoing that we deserved—in our place. And on the other side of the cross, He resurrected to new life, which promises us that we, too, will resurrect one day after death if we trust in Him, for He has fully defeated the thing that causes death: sin.

If you help lead someone to faith in Jesus, the next step is to guide them in prayer. The ministry Cru provides this suggested prayer in accepting Christ as your Savior:

> Lord Jesus, I need you. Thank you for dying on
> the cross for my sins. I open the door of my life
> and receive You as my Savior and Lord. Thank
> You for forgiving my sins and giving me eternal
> life. Take control of the throne of my life. Make
> me the kind of person You want me to be.[6]

Ultimately, how you live your life shares the gospel with those around you. If you aim to live a godly life, others around you can't help but notice the difference in how you speak, act, love, and serve. Inviting people to church, sharing your testimony, investing in getting to know others, praying for them, and meeting their real-life needs all point to Jesus, allowing you to share the truth of the Savior.

Sabbath

> Remember the Sabbath day, to keep it holy:
> You are to labor six days and do all your
> work, but the seventh day is a Sabbath to
> the LORD your God. You must not do any
> work—you, your son or daughter, your male
> or female servant, your livestock, or the
> resident alien who is within your city gates.
> (Exod. 20:8–10)

Girl, you need to rest. Rest from unpacking, rest from creating new relationships, rest from connecting on social media with friends from previous installations, rest from all the phone calls necessary to set up your new life, rest from parenting, rest from work, rest from it all!

In her book *Spiritual Disciplines Handbook*, Adele Calhoun explains sabbath this way:

> As Lord of the sabbath (see Matt. 12:1–14 and
> Luke 6:1–10), he [Jesus] freely interpreted the
> sabbath command, claiming that God gave it to
> people as a restorative and recuperative practice.
> God did not intend for life to be all effort, so he
> punctuated each week with twenty-four hours
> of sabbath rest, during which people could
> remember what life is about and who it is for.[7]

God took six days to speak the world into creation, and on the seventh day He rested. When He gave Moses the Ten Commandments, the fourth commanded us to rest, as God did.

Practicing rest is completely countercultural in our society, which tells us busyness and connectivity equate to success. But again, we must intentionally set up our lives in a way that follows and honors the Lord's will for us, even when it doesn't make sense to the world.

This discipline helps us honor God with our time and ensure we recalibrate our lives weekly to His will. Calhoun explains that it's God's way of saying, "Stop. Notice your limits. Don't burn out."[8] As military spouses, we're already living past burnout regularly. So often, we have to bear all the responsibilities on our own, and it's simply too much to never put down.

In starting a practice of sabbath, pick a day of the week that works for you. It doesn't have to be Sunday. Develop a plan with your spouse that enables all members of your family to enjoy the Sabbath. When your husband is gone for work, ask a friend or church member to babysit your kids so you can rest for a few hours.

On your Sabbath day, do what feels rejuvenating for you. Refreshing will be different for all of us based on our personalities. I heard one person say, "If you work with your mind, sabbath with your hands, and if you work with your hands, sabbath with your mind." It may look like reading a book, getting in your garden, taking a nap, going for a hike, or playing an instrument. Also, refrain from checking email and social media and avoid household chores where possible.

Instead, read the Scriptures, listen to worship songs, pray, and enjoy activities that bring you delight. Complete your errands on another day and order dinner in, or make it the day before, so you don't have to work in the kitchen (unless you love cooking). These pieces pull together to enable us to realign our life with God's will and recharge for another week of kingdom work.

Hospitality

Let brotherly love continue. Don't neglect to
show hospitality, for by doing this some have
welcomed angels as guests without knowing it.
(Heb. 13:1–2)

If you never got to call Wally and Bunnie Montgomery your neighbors, I'm so sorry—you missed out. I hadn't previously experienced neighborly hospitality until these two showed up on the doorstep of our dated 1970s lakeside cottage.

After the movers unloaded our boxes in Belton, Texas, Wally and Bunnie came over to welcome us and offer a meal. It wasn't long before they became our surrogate family. They invited us to shows, took us to church, had us over for dinner at least once a week, and watched our dog when we left town. When Tim deployed, Wally hung up our Christmas lights and cared for our lawn. I'd never experienced this level of neighborly care, and you couldn't help but feel the love of Jesus.

Calhoun defines *hospitality* this way: "Hospitality creates a safe, open space where a friend or stranger can enter and experience the welcoming spirit of Christ in another."[9] As followers of Christ, we need to practice this spiritual discipline of hospitality. Of course, certain seasons can make this challenging, like when you have babies and toddlers; that's an excellent time for fellow military spouses to step in and help you. But regardless of the phase of life, you can do things to make people feel welcome.

Hebrews 13:2 states that God wants us to show hospitality to strangers, and in the military, we're constantly coming across new people. Every time we move to a new neighborhood, strangers. Every time we go to the first unit meeting, strangers. Every time we attend a new church, strangers.

Now, I'm not talking about randomly inviting strangers into your home. *Stranger Danger* was a phrase invented for a reason. I mean the people in the military, church, and neighborhood community around you. Take a meal to the family who just welcomed home a baby. Offer to babysit for a friend who needs a break. Invite your new neighbors over for dinner. Host a small Bible study or weekly game night in your home. Invite the neighborhood kids over for an ice cream party or movie night. Think about what you might enjoy doing for others and make it happen.

Finally, you don't need a perfectly decorated or squeaky-clean house to welcome people into your home. Real people live there, and real life happens there. Coming to a place that feels "lived in" can make your guests more comfortable. Remember, hospitality is about opening your doors to show people the love of Jesus, not impressing them with your stuff or housekeeping skills.

Prayer

Pray at all times in the Spirit with every
prayer and request, and stay alert with all
perseverance and intercession for all the saints.
(Eph. 6:18)

Have you seen the movie *War Room*? In the film, the main character's marriage is in crisis when she meets the cutest, most feisty old lady who teaches her about the power of prayer. Part of the movie centers on both women using a prayer closet. I left the movie theater seriously inspired and convicted about my lack of specific, strategic warlike prayer.

As soon as I got home, I went closet to closet, seeing which one I could somehow gut and relocate all the contents. I decided on the coat closet and moved everyone's jackets to the closets in their rooms. Ah, a war room! I printed pictures, inspiring Bible verses, and prayer printables to hang on the walls. I added a pillow, strung up some lights, and brought in some coloring books and crayons for my daughter when she'd inevitably join me in the mornings.

It was a powerful time of growth in my prayer life. I've moved the contents of that prayer closet five times since then. Now, they sit in a neatly organized binder I can pull out and pray over in my living room. As you know, each house has limitations, and a prayer closet was only sometimes an option as we moved. One of my military spouse friends set up a "prayer closet" in her bathroom! Make it work!

Now, the Bible doesn't say you must have a prayer closet; creating one is simply a way to have a focused place to get away with the Lord. Some people love to walk and pray—they feel closest to God while moving in nature. Others like to sing their prayers. Some like to journal their prayers. And others enjoy liturgical prayer (written or memorized prayers). Consider your learning style and what inspires you to help you create the most effective prayer life.

Prayer is both tender and fierce. It connects us in communion and relationship with our heavenly Father. It also serves as ammunition against the enemy whose mission is to kill, steal, and destroy (John 10:10). Sometimes we can overthink prayer, which is a hindrance. We don't have to be fancy or a Bible scholar. We simply need to talk to God like we're talking to a friend. And talk to Him all day long. But what do we talk to Him about?

In Matthew 6:13–19 Jesus provides us a model for prayer. In this famous prayer, Jesus teaches us what our time in prayer should be filled with: praising God, making requests, and asking for forgiveness. We can also fill our prayer time with thanksgiving, a practice of prayer modeled throughout the book of Psalms. Lastly, I implore you to make time to *listen* during prayer. Because prayer is a conversation with God, we need to be still and provide Him the opportunity to speak to us in return.

In 1 Thessalonians 5:17, God tells us to pray without ceasing. Our military life *requires* us to pray at all times to make it through this well. So many things are required of us that we need help to do it all. We must turn to Him constantly throughout the day. And while we watch our fellow military spouses walk through this as well, let's intercede for them in prayer, lifting one another up to the Lord again, and again, and again—without ceasing.

Modeling Jesus: Spiritual Disciplines

Then Jesus left the Jordan, full of the
Holy Spirit, and was led by the Spirit in the
wilderness for forty days to be tempted by

> the devil. He ate nothing during those days,
> and when they were over, he was hungry.
> The devil said to him, "If you are the Son of
> God, tell this stone to become bread."
> (Luke 4:1–4)

To make our time in the military purposeful, we must be diligent in modeling the Messiah. In the above verses, we witness Him practicing a few spiritual disciplines (memorization of God's Word, fasting, and praying). However, I'm sure He practiced many more during His time in the desert, such as worship, teachability, unplugging, mindfulness, discernment, silence, submission, waiting, meditation, and more.

After Jesus's baptism, God led Him into the desert to prepare Him for his next three years of ministry before Jesus's impending sacrifice on the cross. While Jesus was there, the enemy swooped in to try to tempt Jesus, just as he did with Adam and Eve. However, Jesus was equipped with the Word of God and used that to battle the enemy's suggestion to eat on His fast.

Have you ever fasted before? It's a spiritual practice I'm learning to implement in my life, but the longest I've gone so far is thirty-six hours, and I was *starving*. I cannot fathom how physically, emotionally, and mentally weak Jesus must have been during his forty-day fast. Remember, He was human at this point, feeling all the emotions we experience as humans. Yet He was not spiritually weak because He equipped Himself with God's truth.

What a lesson we can learn from the Savior! Move after move and disappointment after disappointment, this military life regularly leads me to physical, emotional, and mental weakness. And the *only thing* that inspires me to keep battling the enemy's attempts to defeat me is my faith in Jesus and the Word of God.

Prayer

Dear Heavenly Father,

Thank You for showing me what it looks like to love You and follow Jesus. Help me put spiritual disciplines into practice that lead me to live a God-honoring life. Lord, create an insatiable desire to read Your Word daily. Help me see how the Scriptures offer hope and peace amid the perpetual trials and chaos I face as a military wife. Lead my family to a church that glorifies You, God, and help us create relationships with those who can support us in this unpredictable life. Show me how I can serve my local church, Lord, and help me use the gifts You've given me. God, help me open my home and reflect Your love to my community. And help me meet with You in prayer every day, all day. In Jesus's faithful name, amen.

Reflection Questions

1. Is something holding you back from being an all-in follower of Jesus? If so, what needs to change to help you overcome this obstacle?

2. If God invited you to sit down with Him for a loving conversation today, what do you think He might say to you, and what would you ask Him?

3. Is church an integral part of your life? Why or why not? If not, ask God to lead you to the right church for your family. Your unit chaplain can help you find one if needed.

4. Where do you have time in your daily schedule to read the Bible? Is there something you need to cut out to make room for God's Word?

5. Do you regularly practice the sabbath? If not, how could you practically add this spiritual discipline to your life?

6. In what ways can you show your neighbors and community the love of Christ through your hospitality?

7. What does your prayer life look like on a day-to-day basis? Do you need to do anything to activate or enhance it?

―――――――――――― *Next Steps* ――――――――――――

❑ Research local churches in your area.
❑ Contact the church volunteer coordinator and ask how you can serve.
❑ Join a Bible study, life group, or small group (by yourself, with your spouse, or with your whole family).
❑ Find a Christian mentor to guide you and hold you accountable.
❑ Pray daily.
❑ Read the Bible daily (you can use a Bible reading plan—there are many on the Internet).
❑ Identify a day to sabbath each week.

❑ Think about ways to share the gospel with people you're in relationship with.

❑ Download a Bible reading app (Dwell or YouVersion).

❑ Watch the movie *War Room*.

Resources

For links and descriptions of each resource, visit Ashleyashcraft.com/missionreadymarriage.

- The Bible
- Cadence International
- Cru Military
- Protestant Women of the Chapel (PWOC)
- MilSpo. Co.
- Armed Services Ministry
- Navigators Military
- *How to Read the Bible for All It's Worth* by Gordon D. Fee and Douglas Stuart
- *Women of the Word* by Jen Wilken
- *The Bible Recap* by Tara Leigh Cobble
- *What Is a Healthy Church?* by Mark Denver
- *A Praying Life* by Paul E. Miller
- *Spiritual Disciplines Handbook* by Adele Calhoun
- *Spiritual Disciplines for the Christian Life* by Donald Whitney
- *A Short Guide to Spiritual Disciplines* by Mason King

- *The Discipline of Grace* by Jerry Bridges
- *Habits of Grace* by David Mathis
- *Encountering God* by Kelly Minter
- *What Is the Gospel?* by Greg Gilbert
- *Praying Women* by Sheila Walsh
- *Experiencing Prayer with Jesus* by Henry and Norman Blackaby
- *Rule of Life* podcast
- *Dr. James Dobson's Family Talk* podcast
- *Daily Grace* podcast
- *BibleProject* podcast
- 9marks.org
- thegospelcoalition.org/churches
- Practicing the Way

Chapter Five

Enemy: Understanding and Defeating the Liar

I tend to believe my husband is the enemy
when _____.

I can't do this. I can't do this. The phrase rhythmically repeated with each crunch of my camel-colored boots as I walked out to the curb in front of the log cabin we called home. When I reached the end of the snowplow-scraped gravel road, I set down the delicate pink piano my children joyfully tinkered on since the days they gained enough strength to pull themselves to standing on their chubby baby feet.

And then I left it there, on the melting snow-puddled road, next to our tan suede couch, mattresses, garbage bags filled with all our clothes, the hand-painted Scripture sign our children's godmother made, and every other porous item in our house.

My insides squeezed with pain in protest as I left each item to be tossed into a garbage truck and carelessly crushed with no regard to the memories they contained. I put my mask back on in defeat and plodded back up the hill to grab the next armful of cherished items bound for the same landfill while my husband watched our kids in our new barren condo.

Before we switched child-watching duties back at the condo, I stripped off the clothes I'd contaminated and changed into something safe. A mold assessor had called me up to the attic one month prior: "You're going to want to see this." Penicillium-aspergillus filled the attic, a neurotoxic mold. He announced the same frightening findings in the crawl space, the basement, the bedrooms, the living room, the playroom—everywhere. Over the last two years, none of the tens of medical specialists attributed our ailments to mold. Now that we knew *mold* was the culprit of our sickness, doctors and remediators advised us to dispose of everything we owned.

In the quiet of the night, on a blowup mattress borrowed by friends, the enemy tried to sneak in and begin his game of destruction. *It's Tim's fault. You wouldn't be here if he had left the Army after his initial commitment like you pleaded with him to do. Your kids wouldn't be gasping for breath in the middle of the night and battling the effects of brain damage. Your husband should have listened to you.* Like the maliciously crafted lie Satan uttered to make Eve doubt God's goodness, the enemy tried to use the same tactic on me.

But God. Because I knew how the enemy operated and because I studied the Scriptures, I could quiet the lies and not give in to the enemy's temptations to believe my husband was to blame. Reciting the Word of God and remembering His promises caused the evil one to flee.

Can you imagine the destruction Satan could have caused in my family if I believed his lies in the midst of throwing everything we owned on the curb, the financial burden of refurnishing another home, dragging my kids from doctor's appointment to doctor's appointment, and constantly meeting with lawyers and insurance companies? Despite the overwhelming stressors that season, our faith in God increased, and our marital relationship deepened significantly. The enemy could not get a hold on us, although he tried!

I'm about to ask you a serious and possibly painful question. After I ask it, I want you to sit with it for a moment; don't move on immediately. Does the enemy have a hold on you or your marriage?

Now, say this prayer: "Dear God, please reveal to me any areas of my marriage where I view my husband as the enemy." Be still for a few minutes, and let God speak to you before you keep reading.

A Psychologist's View of Satan

A psychologist studies someone's mind and behavior. So let's pretend Satan is sitting in our proverbial chair for a moment and get to understand who he is and how he operates. Just as our husbands study their enemy during combat, we, too, must learn to study our enemy. Do not be fooled into thinking the devil is some mythical creature. The Bible tells us he is very real.

As is true of all doctor visits, we must begin by listing his name on the intake form. All of his names wouldn't fit on the form's line. Here is a list of some of the names given to our enemy: the devil (Heb. 2:14), the serpent (Gen. 3:1), Lucifer (Isa. 14:12 KJV), the evil one (1 John 2:13–14), tempter (Matt. 4:3), ruler of the demons (Mark 3:22), murderer (John 8:44), adversary

(1 Pet. 5:8), deceiver of the whole world (Rev. 12:9), accuser of our brothers and sisters (Rev. 12:10), and Satan (Zech. 3:1).

Before God cast Satan out of heaven, he originally resided as an exquisite angel in God's heavenly kingdom and was named Lucifer, meaning "day star" or "son of the morning." The prophet Ezekiel records God's proclamation about this magnificent cherub He created (who ultimately turned against his Creator) (Ezek. 28:13–15).

In his free will, Lucifer fell victim to pride, idolizing his God-given wisdom and beauty. Both 2 Peter 2:4 and Revelation 12:4 testify that other angels were also cast out of heaven for their sins. Thankfully, God is omnipotent (all-powerful), and Satan's attempt to overthrow the Almighty was in vain. No one can usurp the Lord's authority on the throne.

Understanding the enemy's background gives us precious information in learning his character, which is steeped in pride. When we look at every type of sin committed, pride is always at the root. This is true for Satan and ourselves. When this coup occurred, God threw Lucifer and the offending angels out of heaven.

Now, Lucifer is sentenced to a life outside of God's kingdom. Peter warns us that the enemy prowls the earth like a roaring lion looking for someone to devour (1 Pet. 5:8). His first victims were Adam and Eve, falling prey to his questions that led them to doubt our good God's plan to protect them.

God's commands are in place to protect us from ourselves. When he told Adam and Eve not to eat from the tree of good and evil, He wasn't holding out on them, trying to keep them from joy and pleasure. He was protecting them from knowing sin, pain, evil, and death. However, in his crafty use of language,

Satan twisted God's words ever so slightly, convincing the first man and woman it was okay to disobey God.

And you know what happened next. Adam and Eve were exiled from the garden. This was also an act of God's protection so they would not eat from the tree of life (Gen. 3:22). Had they eaten from the tree of life in their fallen condition, they would have stayed in that condition immortally, and by extension, the rest of humankind after them would have to live forever on this sin-soaked planet. No thank you.

The Enemy's Tactics to Destroy You

Lies

John 8:44 tells us an essential truth about Satan: "He was a murderer from the beginning, not holding to the truth, for there is no truth in him. When he lies, he speaks his native language, for he is a liar and the father of lies" (NIV). How can you know when the enemy is trying to lie to you? The answer is easy: what he says does not line up with God's Word.

Here's the catch. To know the *lies* of Satan, you have to know the *truth* of God's Word. That means you have to study the Bible. We must be intimately familiar with our heavenly Father to protect ourselves from the father of lies. We can do this by reading the Bible daily, joining a Bible study, attending church, and listening to online sermons and Bible podcasts.

However, you can't rely on your pastor or a podcast to teach you about God's truths once a week. Instead, find ways to submerge yourself in the Bible, learning, memorizing, and meditating on God's truths, so you can immediately pick up on any false spin the enemy attempts to trick you into believing.

Discord in Relationships

Unfortunately, I'm pretty good at cooperating with the enemy. Stress, sleep deprivation, hunger, or constant inconvenient news from Uncle Sam are all triggers that may evoke a non-God-honoring response, whether toward my husband or my kids. Instead of responding in gentleness or respect, I can partner with Satan and disobey how God calls me to respond—in grace and love.

In Ephesians 4:26–27, Paul writes that if we let the sun go down on our anger, we give the devil a foothold. So likewise, if I choose not to forgive my husband, the devil vindictively plants his evil seeds of bitterness and resentment. And I'm sure I don't have to tell you those seeds eventually grow into life-choking weeds.

Now, visualize your husband and yourself as two yellow sunflowers in a garden bed. Then, imagine a rapidly growing weed that intertwines itself around the sunflowers, twisting and pulling them until they begin leaning, bending, and ultimately collapsing under the grip of the weed. Thankfully, if you choose to forgive and offer grace to your spouse, it's like noticing the weed as soon as it sprouts and ripping it out before it can grab onto your stem.

Masquerades as an Angel of Light

The devil doesn't have to work all that hard to identify seemingly innocuous ways to capitalize on our already sinful nature. The light he presents may be "enlightened" teaching or information that pulls us in with a morsel of truth but does not fully align with God's Word, something the world floods us with during this information age.

He may also distract you with the light of busyness, a false sign of success in our modern society. Have you ever been so busy that you didn't have time to pray or read the Bible? I'm talking about a busy lifestyle that leaves no room for God. It's too easy to fill our time with kids' extracurricular activities, serving at church, community groups, and military spouse clubs. These are all good things but not if they take you away from the Lord. As one of my former Bible study leaders used to say, "If you're too busy for God, you're busier than He planned you to be."

As military wives, we endure unique seasons beyond the usual busyness of life that make it a struggle to sit with the Word: in the middle of a move, helping sick kids while solo parenting amid a deployment, caring for a new baby while our husbands are away training in the field. These circumstances are not permanent (although it might feel that way!). A break will come. The move will settle. The baby will grow more independent. This type of military-induced busyness differs from the "successful" busyness I referred to earlier.

Steal, Kill, and Destroy

John 10:10 (ESV) provides critical information about the enemy: "The thief comes only to steal and kill and destroy." For years, I let Satan steal from me. He stole my joy, peace, and trust in God. What a sneaky sucker. And all the while, he tricked me into thinking my husband stole these gifts from me. I'd blame my husband for his nonstop work schedule, the text message interruptions in the middle of the night, the solo parenting I had to do all too frequently, and the empty chair at the dinner table.

In this verse, the Greek word for "kill" is *thyō*, which translates to *sacrifice, slay*, or *slaughter*. This word hits intimately close to home with our husbands' profession, which calls them to be ready to die as a sacrifice for their country. We cannot underestimate the mission of our enemy, yet we're also commanded not to worry or be fearful. God has already defeated death through the sacrifice and resurrection of Jesus. As believers, eternal life with our Father awaits us in heaven.

Apollymi is the Greek word originally used for the word *destroy*, another one of Satan's goals. This word means "to render useless, kill, lose, and put out of the way entirely." That's what he's trying to do to you and your family. If he can get you to doubt your calling as a military wife and a child of God, he can render you useless and put you out of his way, moving on to his next victim.

Thankfully, what comes *immediately* after the frightening news of Satan's attempts to steal, kill, and destroy us in John 10:10 is this truth from Jesus, starting in verse 11 and continuing to verse 15:

> "I am the good shepherd. The good shepherd lays down his life for the sheep. The hired man, since he is not the shepherd and doesn't own the sheep, leaves them and runs away when he sees a wolf coming. The wolf then snatches and scatters them. This happens because he is a hired hand and doesn't care about the sheep. I am the good shepherd. I know my own, and my own

know me, as the Father knows me, and I know
the Father. I lay down my life for the sheep."

Praise the Lord! Although we battle against a real enemy, we
serve an almighty God who promises to protect us, even sacrific-
ing His only Son's life for us.

Where Satan Rules (for Now)

The enemy's power is a fact of life on this side of heaven.
Several places in God's Word acknowledge that Satan is the ruler
of this world (John 12:31–33; 14:30; 16:11; 2 Cor. 4:4; 1 John
5:19); even Jesus Himself says this. After Jesus made his trium-
phal entry into Jerusalem to celebrate Passover (the preface to His
death on the cross later that week), He admitted that His soul
was troubled, anticipating the brutality He was about to endure.

Some Greeks and disciples gathered around Jesus when a
voice from heaven responded, proclaiming that God's name
would be glorified. John 12:30–31 (NIV) says, "This voice was
for your benefit, not mine. Now is the time for judgment on this
world; now the prince of this world will be driven out." Here,
Jesus confirms that Satan is the ruler of this world *and* that we
do not need to fear because Jesus's authority and gospel work will
cast out the devil.

God has ultimate authority over everything, even the world
Satan temporarily holds under his sway. Our God can overturn
the enemy's schemes at any point. And He gives us plenty of
battle armor to fight the enemy, too (see Eph. 6). Sometimes,
however, God allows our battle with the enemy to rage far longer than we'd prefer. This was the case with Jesus in His own

temptation during His time in the wilderness (Matt. 4:1–11), and it is true of our wilderness seasons as well. While these seasons of battle seem confusing to our little three-pound brains, we cannot see the complete picture. We can turn to the book of Job for an example of what it looks like when Satan tries to pull us away from the Lord, yet we find great hope in how the Lord redeems and uses every challenge we endure if we partner with Him.

Please note the Scriptures say God will *test* our faith (Deut. 8:2–5), but He will never *tempt* us to sin (James 1:13). There's a significant difference there!

Although we can't fully comprehend the ways of the enemy, we can find peace in the knowledge that the end of his reign was already determined in the first book of the Bible. In Genesis 3:15, God states to Satan, "I will put enmity between you and the woman, and between your offspring and her offspring; he shall bruise your head, and you shall bruise his heel" (ESV). This verse is called the *protoevangelium,* which means "first gospel proclamation." Here, God reveals that the child (Jesus) of a woman will one day defeat the devil.

In Revelation, the last book of the Bible, we see a glimpse of how it's all going to end one day: "The devil who deceived them was thrown into the lake of fire and sulfur where the beast and the false prophet are, and they will be tormented day and night forever and ever" (Rev. 20:10). His end is cemented; our victory is already won.

As followers of Jesus, Satan may have the temporary power to tempt us, distract us, lie to us, or oppress us, but he no longer has the power to *force* us to sin or pull us into hell. We belong to our heavenly Father, and when we cease to inhale another breath, we can trust that one day we will live with God in the new heaven and new earth where we receive a fully renewed body and spirit (Rev. 21:1–4; Phil. 3:21). My questions about the enemy's power find rest in trusting God. That's a significant part of faith. There are things I cannot comprehend, but I understand the heart of my God, and I believe His promise in Romans 8:28 that He works everything for good for those who love Him and are called according to His purposes.

The Enemy in Your Marriage

In a spin-off of C. S. Lewis's *The Screwtape Letters* (a famous satire about a veteran devil who teaches a novice devil how to tempt humans), Kelsey Shade writes a version titled "A Screwtape Letter for the Underappreciated Mom," in which she gives us a glimpse into how the enemy can work in our marriages. Below, the experienced devil is talking to his protégé.

> A word of caution here. Remember, the love of a husband can be dangerous to our cause. If he senses her unhappiness, he may begin to help or (even worse) show her affection. This is where previously planted seeds of resentment can be guided into full bloom. Make her think that his displays of affection are because he "only wants one thing." Do not let her view his help with the dishes (or kisses or cuddling) as having pure motives. If he shows his desire for her, convince her that she is being used, not loved. As we both know, the ultimate Act of Marriage can bond them together in a way that can undo

much hard work on our part. Because of this,
do not allow her to prioritize that Act on her
mental to-do-list. It is in our best interest to
keep the wife busy, busy, busy and be sure she's
far too exhausted to consider it by the end of
the evening.[1]

Does any of this sound familiar to you? These thoughts
are way too convicting for my comfort! They feel like a mirror reflecting the regular unguarded thoughts in my mind.
Because I naturally struggle with these thoughts, I've memorized
Philippians 4:8 as a weapon against the enemy's attempts to keep
me stuck there: "Finally brothers and sisters, whatever is true,
whatever is honorable, whatever is just, whatever is pure, whatever is lovely, whatever is commendable—if there is any moral
excellence and if there is anything praiseworthy—dwell on these
things." I repeat this verse and follow its instructions until I'm
back in God's will, taking my thoughts captive (2 Cor. 10:5).

Another way we can stand firm against the enemy's schemes
is to daily put on the full armor of God, explained in Ephesians
6:11–17 (NLT):

Put on all of God's armor so that you will be
able to stand firm against all strategies of the
devil. For we are not fighting against flesh-
and-blood enemies, but against evil rulers and
authorities of the unseen world, against mighty
powers in this dark world, and against evil spirits in the heavenly places.

Therefore, put on every piece of God's
armor so you will be able to resist the enemy

in the time of evil. Then after the battle you will still be standing firm. Stand your ground, putting on the belt of truth and the body armor of God's righteousness. For shoes, put on the peace that comes from the Good News so that you will be fully prepared. In addition to all of these, hold up the shield of faith to stop the fiery arrows of the devil. Put on salvation as your helmet, and take the sword of the Spirit, which is the word of God.

I love how one Christian thinker, Eugene Peterson, paraphrases this for us:

Be prepared. You're up against far more than you can handle on your own. Take all the help you can get, every weapon God has issued, so that when it's all over but the shouting you'll still be on your feet. Truth, righteousness, peace, faith, and salvation are more than words. Learn how to apply them. You'll need them throughout your life. God's Word is an *indispensable* weapon. In the same way, prayer is essential in this ongoing warfare. Pray hard and long. Pray for your brothers and sisters. Keep your eyes open. Keep each other's spirits up so that no one falls behind or drops out. (Eph. 6:13–18 MSG)

Again, we have a choice. Will we wear the armor God provides us or step out into the world unprotected?

Modeling Jesus: Speaking Scripture against the Enemy

The enemy will tempt us to disobey God's will for our lives; we can't get around that fact. He's going to prey on our weaknesses and attack our thoughts. He will try to pit us against our husbands and make us think our service member is the enemy. His mission is our destruction.

But God has given us a way to escape the enemy. He doesn't leave us defenseless. As always, our Father has given us an example through the life of Jesus. Luke 4:1–13 gives us our model for defeating the enemy as we see Jesus do precisely that.

We read a portion of this passage in the last chapter, but this time we're going to look at it from a different angle. In chapter 4, we focused on the *spiritual disciplines* Jesus employed. For the sake of this chapter, we're going to view this section of Scripture through the lens of *defeating the enemy*.

> Then Jesus left the Jordan, full of the Holy Spirit, and was led by the Spirit in the wilderness for forty days to be tempted by the devil. He ate nothing during those days, and when they were over, he was hungry. The devil said to him, "If you are the Son of God, tell this stone to become bread."
>
> But Jesus answered him, "It is written: Man must not live on bread alone."
>
> So he took him up and showed him all the kingdoms of the world in a moment of time. The devil said to him, "I will give you their splendor and all this authority, because it has

been given over to me, and I can give it to anyone I want. If you, then, will worship me, all will be yours."

And Jesus answered him, "It is written: Worship the Lord your God, and serve him only."

So he took him to Jerusalem, had him stand on the pinnacle of the temple, and said to him, "If you are the Son of God, throw yourself down from here. For it is written:

He will give his angels orders concerning you,
to protect you, and
they will support you with their hands,
so that you will not strike
your foot against a stone.

And Jesus answered him, "It is said: Do not test the Lord your God."

After the devil had finished every temptation, he departed from him for a time.

Right after Jesus was baptized and right before He began His official ministry tour (proclaiming the good news of the kingdom of God, offering eternal life for any who would believe in Him, making disciples, and willingly submitting Himself to the cross for our sins), the Holy Spirit led Him to the desert to fast and pray. First, we need to address why Jesus was called to fast. Fasting is a spiritual practice God commands us to do for the benefit of intimate communion with Him. We sacrifice food (or something else) and replace the time we would eat with prayer. Any time we feel hunger pains (or desire to consume what we're fasting from), that's a cue to pray and listen to what God wants to reveal to us. It's a way to help us hunger for God more than we hunger for anything else, and it can also be a way we prepare for important spiritual work.

The first part of this passage is essential: Jesus obeyed the Holy Spirit's leading. We miss God's will for our lives if we don't listen to what the Holy Spirit tells us. I'm guilty of sensing the Spirit's prompting to do something and deciding to stick with my desire.

Satan's first temptation to Jesus is to do something in His own power, outside God's will (vv. 2–3). Sound familiar? This is one of my biggest pitfalls. My innate desire for control constantly tempts me to take care of circumstances in my own power, not trusting God to lead me instead. Second, the enemy pinpointed Jesus's current weakness: hunger. He tried to get Christ to resolve His discomfort. But God's plan was not for Jesus to be comfortable in this moment. His plan was for Jesus to fast in preparation for the critical work ahead.

Did you notice how Jesus responded to the enemy's temptation to disobey God? Jesus cited *Scripture* in response to Jesus's temptations (v. 4). (To explore this further, go back and look at the passage, underlining each time Jesus says, "It is written" or "It is said.") This is key for our defense against the enemy. We have to know the contents of our Bibles. God's Word is our weapon. We need to read it, memorize it, and let it reside within our hearts, ready to be called upon when Satan strikes.

Next, Satan tries to entice Jesus with authority and glory as a means to get Jesus to worship him instead of God (vv. 5–7).

Again, Jesus's first and only response is Scripture (v. 8). The Messiah knows that the right kind of authority and glory is given by God at the right time and in the right way and that human worship belongs to God alone, not Satan.

The last temptation Satan employs to try to trap Jesus asks the Son of God to prove Himself (vv. 8–9). A consistent downfall of many military wives is that we try to prove ourselves, believing we can do it all without help. And when we can't, the enemy steps in to accuse us of our weakness (Rev. 12:10). Thankfully, we can model Jesus's citing of Scripture to defeat the lies of the accuser.

In verses 10 and 11, the enemy uses the same tactic he did in the garden of Eden with Adam and Eve, twisting God's words. And for the final time, Jesus responds to Satan's temptation with Scripture, used in the correct context (v. 12). In each and every temptation the enemy threw at Him, Jesus responded with God's Word. The same should be true of us! Because what *God* says is more powerful than what the enemy says, or what anyone else in this world could say to us. The question is this: *Do we know what God says?* If not, it's time to start getting familiar with our Bible!

As military spouses to our nation's heroes whose sole job is to fight for freedom and protection, I think it's fair to say this lifestyle lends us to a great deal of temptation from the enemy. After all, we're fighting to uphold the value of life and the image of God found in every human being—two things Satan hates. Everything our families stand for, he's attempting to destroy. If Satan can get us to buy into a marital climate of animosity, division, and bitterness, he's accomplished his mission, and we'll do the destructive work for him. It's our job to respond to the enemy's temptations with the Word of God. What God says should end the matter, no matter what. It's the last Word and the only Word that matters. So I'll ask you again: *Do you know it?*

────────────── *Prayer* ──────────────

Dear Heavenly Father,

Thank You for not leaving me defenseless against the enemy that tries to consume me like a roaring lion. You lovingly equip me with Your Word that causes Satan's temptations to cease. Lord, I cannot make the enemy flee in my own strength; I need You. Help me to call on You every time I'm tempted to sin. When I struggle to trust Your words and way, remind me that obeying Your will is the best plan for my life. Thank You for the priceless gift of the Holy Spirit whom You allow to dwell within me, reminding me of Your wisdom so I can successfully live a life that honors You. In this lifestyle where it is easy to blame my spouse for the constant stream of stressors, please help me remember Your truth in Ephesians 6:12, which tells me I do not battle against people but the spiritual forces of evil. And God, help me not to fear the enemy, recalling that You tell me to be strong and courageous, not to fear or be discouraged, because You are with me wherever I go (Josh. 1:9). In Jesus's powerful name, amen.

────────────── *Reflection Questions* ──────────────

1. In what ways are you tempted to believe that Satan's work in your life isn't real or isn't that bad? How do the passages explored in this chapter speak to this?

2. Identify the areas of your life where you notice the enemy tries to attack you the most frequently.

3. Are there underlying hurts or past trauma in the above-listed areas you need help processing so you can move toward healing? If so, what next steps can you take to seek help?

4. Does anything about your husband's job lead to falsely identifying him as the enemy (excessive work hours, deployments, frequent moves, talking to you like you are one of his unit members, etc.)? Reread Ephesians 6:12 in multiple translations (try NLT, ESV, CSB, and NIV). Now try to put the verse in your own words. What does this verse remind you of in the moments you see your husband as the enemy?

5. Which piece of the armor of God is hardest for you to "put on" each day? Why? Which is easiest?

6. Do you regularly practice memorizing Scripture to defend yourself against the enemy? If yes, what verses are the most helpful for you? If not, look up some helpful Bible verses in the areas you struggle with and write them down.

Next Steps

- ❏ Identify and memorize Scripture verses to defeat the enemy when he tries to tempt you.
- ❏ Pray when you need God's help to avoid the enemy's snares.
- ❏ Seek professional Christian counseling for past issues that make you vulnerable to the enemy's attacks.

❑ Ask a Christian friend to be an accountability and prayer partner, someone safe and
trustworthy to whom you can confess your
sins and request prayer when the enemy
attacks.

Resources

For links and descriptions of each resource, visit
Ashleyashcraft.com/missionreadymarriage.

- *When the Enemy Strikes* by Charles Stanley
- *The Screwtape Letters* by C. S. Lewis
- "A Screwtape Letter for the Unappreciated
  Mom" by Kelsey Shade
- *The Bondage Breaker* by Neil Anderson
- *The Adversary* by Mark Bubeck
- *Don't Give the Enemy a Seat at Your Table*
  by Louie Giglio
- *The Armor of God* by Priscilla Shirer

Chapter Six

Family: Learning to Understand One Another

One way my family and/
or in-laws support us well is
by _____.

In the early years of my marriage, I didn't know how to work through disagreements in a healthy way. I was a runner. It was like my inner child wanted to pack a box of cookies and a spare set of clothes, stuff them into a blanket and secure my necessities around a stick, marching off, declaring my power to escape any uncomfortable situation.

I recall one occasion in Alabama when Tim and I had an argument, and I grabbed the keys to my white Volvo S60 and drove off without telling him where I was going. Enterprise, Alabama, is a stereotypical small Southern town, one you'd hear about in a country song, so there wasn't anywhere to escape. I actually drove past Tim in his navy blue Ford Explorer trying to find me. My cheeks blushed in embarrassment at my childish escapade, and I returned to our old brick home, realizing how unhelpful my dramatic exit proved to be in working through our disagreement.

Why did I feel the need to leave each time my husband offended me or disagreed with me, whether that was storming off to our bedroom and shutting the door behind me or driving away? Years later, after working through some of my challenges with a Christian counselor, I finally began to understand myself for the first time. *That's why!* She helped me get to the root causes of my issues, something I couldn't figure out alone.

Doing the Hard Work of Understanding Yourself First

Before we can work to understand our spouses and families (which leads us to love them in a God-honoring way), we have to look at ourselves. Human beings are complicated! You are complicated. I am complicated. Our spouses are complicated. Our families of origin are complicated. Our extended families are complicated. The families we marry into are complicated.

As such, having relationships with others is often messy and painful. However, if we genuinely understand how God created us as individuals, we can more effectively work through selflessly serving and extraordinarily loving those around us. When we can identify our weaknesses, cultivate our strengths, and know what it takes to operate as our best selves, we're on the way to loving others as Jesus did.

Sin Bents

The sinful aspects of our character need attention, so God exposes them with the loving hope that we choose to partner with Him in removing these negative characteristics and habits from our lives. But unfortunately, pride often makes us blind to our sins. Have you ever gotten defensive when your spouse brings up something about you that's bothering him? Well, that's pride: the root of all sin. It feels easier—and dare I say, good—to hang on to those comfortable sinful bents outside God's will for us.

Thankfully, marriage brings out the worst in us. *Wait! What?* Why would we be grateful that marriage reveals our dark and sometimes hidden nature? Because one way God uses marriage is to shine a light on our sins so we can start dealing with them. When married, we can't hide those things outside God's will. Marriage is the Great Exposer.

Think of it this way: if there's a certain kind of cancer, disease, or broken bone in your body, you want to know about it, right? Going to the radiology unit and getting the X-ray or the MRI can be annoying, time-consuming, or even painful, but it's worth it. Why? Because getting the imaging done lets you see the problem for what it is. Marriage is like that some days. It reveals the issues on the inside. And blaming the *marriage* for your internal issues isn't going to work any more than blaming an X-ray for a broken bone. We've all got broken parts inside of us, spiritually and emotionally speaking. And we all need God to help us see those things when we're blind to them. So, why not let God use marriage in the restorative way He's designed it? Why not let marriage reveal any broken, wounded, or sinful issues inside of you so you can pinpoint them and heal?

I want to offer you a dare, which will force you to be vulnerable with your spouse. When the conditions are as close to right as possible (they'll never be perfect in this military lifestyle), tell your husband that you're permitting him to expose your blind spots—sinful habits or attitudes you can't see. He might think you've gone a little crazy, but express your seriousness. Remember: everyone's got internal, hidden issues. You're not the exception, and neither am I. Our choice isn't between whether or not there's something inside we need to deal with; it's between whether or not we'll join God in healing what is most certainly already there.

One of our goals in marriage is to help each other grow into who God designed us to be. But we can't do that without working through the parts of our character that don't align with the Son of God. We can't do this alone, but we can hand our sin bents over to God and ask Him to lead us toward freedom. By studying His Word, obeying His commands, and spending time in prayer, we welcome the Holy Spirit to begin transforming our hearts.

Personality Type

Humans have derived many tests and terms to define ourselves: Myers-Briggs Type Indicator; 16 Personalities; DISC Assessment; The Big 5; StrengthsFinder; and Type A, B, C, and D Personalities are some of the more popular. While I'm not endorsing any of these tests, I believe it's essential to identify some of these basic elements of ourselves so we can communicate them to our families.

For example, let's look at the introvert/extrovert personality type. As military wives, this is an important aspect of our personalities we need to communicate to our husbands due to all the social functions we are expected to attend (like change of command ceremonies, hail and farewell events, family readiness group meetings, holiday parties, and formals). Our personality types also come into play when it's time to move, which forces us to meet new people and develop relationships regularly.

My husband could not be more extroverted. He loves gathering with others, trying new things, and feels energized after spending time with people. So, for several years, he didn't understand why I wasn't excited to attend all his military events. As an ambivert (did you know that was a thing?), I can hang with him at social functions for about an hour and a half, and then I'm completely drained. Tim gets energized by being around people, but I recharge by spending time alone or with a small group of close friends.

Knowing this about ourselves helps in all facets of marriage. It plays out in our daily decisions and special family times like vacations. When Tim and I go on vacation, we've learned that he wants to visit museums, read each historical marker, and explore every highlighted attraction. Me? I'd rather relax on the beach or casually stroll in a beautifully landscaped garden. So now we make sure to do both.

Your Triggers

Before marriage, I didn't understand what "triggers" meant. But after spending time with two Christian counselors, I learned the importance of this word. When we experience a trigger, something attached to a painful or traumatic memory takes us back to that event. It could be a smell, a comment, a sight, or a word. Identifying and explaining your triggers to your husband is imperative for intimacy in your marriage.

You may need help from a professional Christian counselor to do this. To help you identify your triggers (if any), ask yourself these questions: What makes me angry? What makes me fearful? What makes me anxious? Then, fill in your answers below, and share them with your husband. Here are some examples to get you started:

Triggers	Source
When people lie to me	Someone I trusted as a child lied regularly
When I don't hear from my husband shortly after he predicted landing from his night flight	Soldiers we know have died in helicopter crashes
When my family leaves their belongings strewn around the house	I grew up in a home that was always kept tidy

Love Languages

What makes you feel loved? When my husband puts away all other distractions, locks eyes with me, and talks about something meaningful, that's what does it for me. But Tim doesn't need quality time the same way I do. Instead, he feels loved when I speak his love language of physical touch. Thankfully, we learned about Dr. Gary Chapman's book, *The 5 Love Languages*, early in our marriage. This simple yet profound knowledge could revolutionize your marriage.

Through counseling married couples, many of whom were military couples, Dr. Chapman discovered that there are five primary love languages: acts of service, words of affirmation, quality time, physical touch, and receiving gifts. It's essential to know which type your husband is so you can love him in a way that he actually *feels* loved (as opposed to only showing love the way *you'd* want to experience it). And the same is true in reverse; it's essential for your husband to know your primary love language so his efforts to show affection are effective.

However, as a military couple, implementing these love languages becomes challenging when you throw in deployments and training away from home. Thankfully, Gary Chapman and Jocelyn Green wrote a military edition of *The 5 Love Languages* that provides a host of ways to prioritize one another's love language even when physical separation occurs. If you and your spouse haven't explored your love languages, I encourage you to do so!

Reflecting on Your Family of Origin (and His)

Much of what we learn about marriage comes from our families of origin, whether positive or negative. Both husband and wife bring different experiences, hurts, and expectations to a marriage. Understanding our partner's family helps us communicate and support each other more effectively. Below are a few questions you can ask each other and space to record your answers.

- What were your favorite childhood experiences that you want to replicate in our family?

   Your answer:

   His answer:

- What did you appreciate about your mom's role as a wife and mother?

   Your answer:

   His answer:

- What do you wish she would have done differently?

   Your answer:

   His answer:

- What did you appreciate about your dad's role as a husband and father?

   Your answer:

   His answer:

- What do you wish he would have done differently?

   Your answer:

   His answer:

- What parts of your childhood were painful?

   Your answer:

   His answer:

Finally, you don't have to repeat the patterns of your parents if they did not have a God-honoring marriage. You didn't have a say in the marriage (or lack thereof) you were exposed to as a child, but you are responsible for *your* marriage. It is exciting, even exhilarating, that we can model godly marriages to our children, teaching them what it looks like to serve and love selflessly. Our commitment to *work* toward God-honoring marriages will transform the generations who come after us. Amazing!

Family Vision

We can't change the past in our family of origin (and maybe you wouldn't want to!), but a beautiful part of your marriage is that God has allowed you to cast a new vision. Incorporate what worked from your family and his, and eliminate what didn't. Genesis 2:24 tells us that we are supposed to leave our father and mother and cleave to our new family. So, what are your hopes, dreams, and prayer for *your* marriage and family?

As an adult, I've heard various Christians discuss their vision for their family. What is a vision? A vision defines your purpose and long-term goals. You can do this as an individual, couple, or family. As believers in Christ, our visions should be centered on the truths of God's Word. Identify some Bible verses you gravitate toward and incorporate them into your vision. You might want to create a family vision statement and choose a passage you identify as your family verse.

Here are a couple of real vision statements from fellow military families.

- "To demonstrate God's love by making the most of every opportunity."—Juergens family[2]

- "We follow Christ together, joining Jesus in His mission by loving sacrificially, listening attentively, focusing on the wildly important, and becoming sturdy men and women of God."—Vaughan family
- "We work together to use our gifts to love one another and bear each other's burdens, honoring God and each other. We show hospitality and build community wherever we go. Our priorities are faith, family, and flag."—Gawlikowski family
- "Live like Jesus: be the first to serve, and never walk past a problem."—Bailey family

Complications of Extended Family amid Military Life

Unfortunately, families of origin are a common source of strife in military marriages. I've heard this again and again from fellow military spouses. Earlier this year, I asked a dear friend about her biggest challenge as a military wife. Under the shade of a rainbow-colored beach umbrella, while our kids splashed in the lake, tears slid down her cheeks. After informing her family they wouldn't be able to travel home for a visit, her parents placed undeserved shame on her in response to her husband's military duty.

If you're new to the military, you might experience some of the following challenges, and if you're a seasoned military spouse, you may be all too familiar with these difficulties. I asked my military spouse friends about the challenges they've experienced regarding extended family, and here's what they said:

"There is always the expectation that all leave should mean trips home. We rarely took a family vacation that wasn't to visit family."

"We're always expected to travel far. We had come to the States to visit for a family reunion. Still, even our family who lives stateside won't travel to the family reunion site because it's 'too far.' I've gone years without seeing my extended family because they weren't willing to come to visit me in my home because we were too 'far away,' yet we are expected to visit 'home.' The family will not meet us in the middle."

"Only share your marital problems with people who won't hold anything against you or your husband. Oftentimes at the beginning of my marriage, I would call home and tell my mom everything. Later, my husband and I would grow and learn how to fix our issues, but my mom would still hold on to what I told her."

"I struggle with traveling home to see both sides of the family. We 'need' to be the ones traveling to see every individual, even when we've flown across the globe with five small children. Additionally, our families are states apart, and visiting one family and not both is always seen as a competition."

"The questions! 'When are you moving back home?' However, 'home' has never been on our radar to return to, military or not. Also, when my spouse has leave, they ask, 'How long will you be visiting for?' Well, what if we want to take our kids on an exciting vacation? We always get guilt-tripped into having to take his time off to go back and see family. Once there, we must drive all over, splitting the time equally not to hurt anyone."

"A big one we are currently facing overseas is communication. Some families refuse to use technology. I get it, technology isn't always favorable, although how awesome is it that we can keep in touch in real time these days? It is devastating when our family refuses to use it and then blames you for keeping their grand-kids away from them."

"My extended family doesn't always get that we make friends who are like family at almost every duty station. I feel like our family who isn't military doesn't understand this and feels replaced. We need to make our home wherever the military sends us, not where we grew up. I think that's hard for them."

I want to share some other challenges you may face regarding extended families, ones I didn't anticipate.

When your husband returns home from deployment, you may be inclined to pull out *all* the stops and invite *all* the family. If my son deployed for a year, I'd want to see him the *second* he was home! However, after a long or traumatic deployment, the extra company, stimulation, conversations, and questions may be too much for your husband to process upon stepping off the plane. So before inviting others to welcome-home ceremonies, speak with your spouse, consider his personality type, and weigh the pros and cons of an immediate (or surprise) visit with family.

Another challenge you may face when it comes to extended families is financial strain. Depending on where you are stationed, it may be impossible to travel home due to cost. Tim and I recently looked at plane tickets to take our family of five home for Christmas. Five plane tickets from North Carolina to Arizona cost five thousand dollars! Needless to say, we stayed at Fort Liberty to celebrate the birth of Christ.

Helping Our Families Understand Military Life

Now that we've addressed some of the difficulties we may encounter with our relatives, I want to make sure we discuss how to help them understand our challenges and ways they can assist us as military families.

How Military Families Can Help Their Extended Family Members

- Share books, podcasts, posts, magazines, movies, and articles that provide helpful information and perspective. You can download a free suggested resource list to share with your loved ones at ashleyashcraft .com/missionreadymarriage.

- Lovingly provide transparent information about your family's needs in that season. For example: "We would love to see you right now, but we haven't had alone time with Tim in months, and we need a few days to create memories together as a family. Can you visit next month instead?" Or, "I'm so sorry we can't travel home for the holidays. We all enjoy celebrating with you but cannot afford plane tickets this year."

- Keep them in the know. Share pertinent unit information, dates, and events, such as training exercises, deployments, and fundraisers they may want to support. However, do not share any information that violates operational security (OPSEC).

- Invite them to military events they can attend, like reenlistment ceremonies, changes of command, memorial services, holiday unit parties, and MWR (Moral, Welfare, and Recreation) events.

- Plan at least one visit home per year, if possible.

- Call home at regular intervals (my rule of thumb is at least once a week, but every family is different). If you have kids, video chat is beneficial to keep the connection. (Remembering to contact family starts as a habit you may have to reinforce by using alarms or digital schedule reminders; over time it will become more natural.)

- Explain what communications will be like during training or deployments to the best of your knowledge. For example, "Tim won't be able to contact anyone while out in the field for two weeks." Or, "Tim may be able to call you once a month on his deployment."

Modeling Jesus: Embracing Your Spiritual Family

So, what do we do when our extended families don't get it right? When they don't understand our lifestyle? When they do not forgive our circumstances? When they blame and shame us for situations that are ultimately in the military's control? And what do we do when we feel like we need the support and encouragement of our family, but they're across the ocean, country, or state lines? What do we do? We look to Jesus, the One God calls us to emulate.

> While he was still speaking with the crowds, his mother and brothers were standing outside wanting to speak to him. Someone told him, "Look, your mother and your brothers are standing outside, wanting to speak to you."
> He replied to the one who was speaking to him, "Who is my mother and who are my brothers?" Stretching out his hand toward his disciples, he said, "Here are my mother and my

brothers! For whoever does the will of my Father
in heaven is my brother and sister and mother."
(Matt. 12:46–50)

When Jesus's mother and brothers sought his attention, He
was preaching to a crowd that included Pharisees and teachers
of the law about evil spirits and the wickedness of the generation. We know that Jesus had earthly brothers and sisters born
to Mary and Joseph, as stated in Matthew 13:55. We don't know
why they wanted to see Jesus at this point, but what I want to
highlight is his definition of family.

I want you to visualize this beautiful verse. Picture yourself
in a crowd surrounding Jesus on the Sabbath. You're standing
on a dusty road under the shade of a cypress tree, and the stale
stench of men and animal dung hangs in the air. Or maybe, the
aroma of bread and fig cakes wafts around them as they con-
gregate outside a family's home. (Let's go with the latter!) The
fatigue from teaching crowds all day begins to show in Christ's
posture, and His eyes appear heavy. Yet He opens his arms wide
in love, proclaiming His *disciples* are His family. Your heart swells
in awe that the Son of God calls *you* His sister.

Jesus tells us that our family bloodline is not the sole determining boundary marker in our familial borders. As believers,
the Son of God says that our family comprises "whoever does
the will of my Father in heaven." This is news worth celebrating as military wives. God doesn't leave us to care for ourselves
when we're far away from the "village" we were born in. We
have fathers, mothers, sisters, and brothers wherever the military
takes us.

When your mom doesn't live nearby, the wise woman in your Bible study can step in to love on you. When your dad isn't physically close and you need help while your husband is away on duty, you can call on your faithful neighbor across the street. When you wish you could share the struggles of reintegration with your sister, invite the Christ-following mom you met at your kid's soccer practice over for a comforting cup of hot tea.

The key here is that you have to reach out for a connection. As we move around the world, we must stay connected to our family in Christ. Identify the churches you want to try *before* you even move (a blessing in this digital age when you can research churches and listen to the pastor's sermon from anywhere). Get to know your neighbors. Invite new friends for a meal, snacks, or a playdate with your kids. Attend the family support group meetings, join a Bible study on your installation, or become part of the spouse's club. However you do it, connections to your spiritual family are vital.

I want to conclude this chapter with an insightful commentary from Chuck Smith. See the following words through the lens of the military.

> Now it is true, that those who have a bond in Christ, those who are related by Jesus Christ, have a closer relationship then [sic] actual brothers and sisters who are not bound in Christ. In other words, you will have a closer relationship to those in the family of God than to those of your own family, if your own family is not also a part of the family of God. And many of you have no doubt experienced this. Your accepting

of Jesus Christ has created an alienation between some of the members of your own family, blood family. But you've come into a new family, of which ties are deeper and greater, and the bond is tighter. And so with Jesus, His brothers, and all, not believing in Him at that point, said, "who [sic] is my brother? Look, this fellow here, whoever does the will of God, the same is my mother, my sister, my brother."[2]

As I read Chuck's words, my spirit rejoices, and goose bumps rise on my arms. Not only has God gifted me with family in Christ but family in the military. If you allow yourself to connect deeply with the military families God places around you, you will sometimes become closer than family. A deep and undeniable lifelong bond happens within the military community. It's the *best* gift God has given me in this military life. I can see the beloved face of each sister in Christ He's provided for me at every installation, and tears spring forth. He is a good God.

Prayer

Dear Heavenly Father,

I rest in awe of how You expertly and lovingly knitted me and my husband, every fine detail. Help me to have eyes to see the beauty in Your creation of us. How beautiful it is to know that when You wove us in our mothers' wombs, You foreknew we would one day cleave to each other as man and wife. Lord, please help me to learn how my husband desires to be loved. Even when I don't feel like it, give me the nudge to love him in both traditional and creative ways.

And God, I pray the same for my husband—that he would take the time to learn how to love me, becoming a connoisseur of my heart. God, as we become experts in loving each other, please help our extended families to learn how to support and love us well. Remind me to give them grace when they get it wrong. I praise You for creating the opportunity to have new mothers, fathers, brothers, and sisters in Christ. What an undeserved blessing. With the gift of family in mind, please guide my husband and me in creating a godly vision for our family, loving others in Your name, and partnering with You to expand Your kingdom. In Jesus's holy name, amen.

Reflection Questions

1. After you and your husband take the free online love language quiz, record the results below.

My primary love language is:

My husband's primary love language is:

2. Knowing my husband's primary love language, I plan to do the following three things for him within the next week:

-

-

-

3. Describe how your extended family has supported you and/or made things difficult for you since becoming a military spouse.

4. Use this space to brainstorm ideas for your family vision statement. Then, share this with your husband and incorporate his ideas. If you already have one, write it below.

My ideas:

His ideas:

Our family vision statement:

6. Who are some Christ followers you know at your current station who you can ask to support you as family in Christ? If you don't know anyone, how can you meet fellow believers in your local area?

———————————— *Next Steps* ————————————

❏ Complete a personality test.
❏ Make an appointment with a Christian counselor if needed.
❏ Take the free 5 Love Languages test online (and ask your spouse to do it too).
❏ Discuss the questions provided on page 98 with your husband.
❏ Share your top three triggers with your husband, and ask him to share his top three with you. Brainstorm ways the two of you might show sensitivity and care to each other regarding these specific triggers.
❏ Craft a family vision statement and display it on a chalkboard or wall art.
❏ Talk with your extended families about how you might better communicate and support *them*.

❑ After you've asked your extended family how you might better support them, invite them to return the favor, and send them a free list of ways they can support you, found at ashleyashcraft.com/missionreadymarriage.

Resources

For links and descriptions of each resource, visit Ashleyashcraft.com/missionreadymarriage.

- Focus on the Family's nationwide Christian counseling list
- Unit chaplain
- Local pastor
- Military One Source counseling
- *The 5 Love Languages Military Edition* by Gary Chapman and Jocelyn Green
- *Your Family Purpose* course by Dr. Joshua and Christi Straub
- *Take Back Your Family* by Jefferson Bethke
- *Boundaries* by Dr. Henry Cloud and Dr. John Townsend
- *Making Room for Her* by Barbara and Stacy Reaoch
- Focus on the Family Broadcast
- *Family Vision* podcast
- *Building Relationships* podcast

Chapter Seven

Life of a Nomad: Fulfilling Your Calling Where God Places You

The thing I long for the most at my current installation is _____.

Tim knew I wasn't willingly packing for our move to West Point. I may have been rather combatant, in fact. As much as I get satisfaction from crossing things off my to-do list, leaving our desert home wasn't one of the tasks I wanted to check off.

So, as I pulled into the garage of our cream-stuccoed home in Tucson after saying goodbye to my coworkers at the local faith-based pregnancy resource center, resentment toward my husband and this profession of his that kept calling us to leave bubbled to the surface. I found deep purpose and fulfillment in pointing our clients to education and hope, and I wasn't ready to walk away.

Listening to their (often tragic) story, educating them on the options, sharing resources that would enable them to choose life for their baby, and walking them next door to receive a free

ultrasound almost always saved a baby's life. It didn't seem fair
that Tim's job was relocating us when I was partnering with God
to do such meaningful work.

Filled with frustration, I walked through the garage door
attached to our outdated 1970s kitchen, and the most bewilder-
ing sight caught my attention. There were dozens and dozens of
light pink, baby blue, and lavender inflated balloons decorating
our dining room. *Oh, no! Whose birthday did I forget?*

Tim embraced me as I stepped inside, explaining that each
balloon represented a baby I had partnered with God to help
bring to life. There were sixty-two balloons, almost all blue and
pink, representing the baby girls and boys born after their moms
chose life. And a few lavender balloons symbolizing the babies
whose mothers made a different choice, the one that broke my
heart. These balloons represented the babies I would meet once
we're all with God.

Tim's loving gesture that day helped me understand God's
heart, which softened mine. In these moments of confirmation,
I can see a small piece of God's plan for each of our moves. God
didn't need me to stay at the pregnancy resource center, leading
women to choose life for their babies. He was perfectly capable
of calling new workers into that particular field. It was a season.
The visual of those balloons helped me see God's impact through
my work and showed me that was enough. I had fulfilled my
commitment there, and it was time to move on to a new place,
a new mission field, with the same ultimate purpose of sharing
the gospel.

Military Missionaries

I discussed our purpose as military wives earlier. As believers in Christ, we *all* have the same purpose. This purpose holds true no matter what our husbands do for work, whether military members, postal workers, business managers, or teachers. It's the same for your kids who call themselves followers of Christ, and it's the same for your husband if he professes faith in Jesus.

To recall what we learned earlier, Jesus commanded us to *go, make, baptize*, and *teach*. Pastor Greg Laurie explains it this way:

> In Matthew 28:19–20, we find the "marching orders" from Jesus that we know as the Great Commission. There are two things we should remember about it. First, these words are a command. That is why we call it the Great Commission and not the Great Suggestion. Jesus did not say, "Look, if you are in the mood, if it works into your busy schedule, as a personal favor to Me, would you consider going into the world and making disciples?" No. In the original language, this is a command.[1]

You are a military missionary. That statement might feel confusing or shocking, or as it did for me, those words may finally help you accept your place in the military. All of the sacrifice. All of the moving. All of the separations. It's all been for the sake of the gospel and the salvation of the military community where God placed you—and me.

But what is a missionary? A missionary is someone God uses to spread the gospel's message, the good news that there is salvation in Jesus Christ. As believers in Christ, we are all called to do this. In Acts 1:8, Luke tells us that we will receive power when the Holy Spirit comes upon us and that we are to be Christ's witnesses starting at home and moving all the way to the ends of the earth.

Although Jesus said these words to His disciples, He meant them for all His followers. Do you think it's an accident that military families are sent *all* over the world?

The specific way we "go and make disciples" will look different for all of us, but as military spouses, we can share the gospel in some common circles.

Military Discipleship Opportunities

Within each group of people listed below, you can share the gospel and spread Jesus's light through your words and actions. In brief, you can share your testimony, invite them to church or Bible study, pray for them, show kindness, serve them, be generous, and offer grace and forgiveness. Let's look at six groups of people we regularly encounter as military wives and explore how we can share the love and truth of Jesus.

Movers

Most military families regularly encounter movers, whether you're scheduling a moving company, doing a walk-through for an estimate, in the middle of the two days of packing, loading day, coordinating the delivery, or it's finally unloading day. Each of these situations provides you an opportunity to emulate the love and light of Christ.

I have moved twelve times as an Army wife, and I am always saddened when movers comment that being treated kindly is a rarity for them.

Yes, they're going to break some of your belongings. Yes, it might even be your irreplaceable heirlooms. Yes, something will get lost in transit. Yes, they might be smoking in your yard on their break. Yes, you might move faster if you did it yourself with a few friends. But how much more can we share the gospel if we offer kindness, grace, and forgiveness?

Here are some practical things you can do when working with movers:

- Stock your refrigerator with plenty of cold drinks.
- Buy them lunch.
- Say "please" and "thank you" all day.
- Stay calm.
- Offer forgiveness when something inevitably goes wrong (like when the antique fireplace mantel I tediously restored slammed on the ground after the movers left it freestanding in our windy Kansas driveway).
- Give them a generous tip if you can afford it.
- Share your testimony if the opportunity presents itself (how God has transformed or saved you).
- Pray for their salvation.
- In natural conversation, tell them the loss you'll feel about the church you are leaving,

and invite them to go visit the church in your absence, if they are comfortable with that.

- When the job is complete and they are on their way out, ask, "Is there anything I can be praying for in your life?"

Family Support Program

Most of our husbands are in a unit with a family support program. The group typically comprises women volunteering their time as leaders, secretaries, treasurers, and Care Team members. Be intentional about thanking these people for their time and commitment to your unit and family. Some units have amazing support groups, others are practically nonexistent, and some might be drama filled. You can donate your time and talents to help, send thank-you notes after an event they executed, invite them to your Bible study or church, or have them over for a meal.

Neighbors

As you know, God determines our exact address, which means He places us next to our neighbors on purpose. When we lived on Fort Leavenworth, we lived in a cul-de-sac with four homes. Within those four homes resided *eighteen* children. Yes, you read that right. During that time, God blessed us with beautiful friendships (for both the adults and the kids). We all took turns babysitting one anothers' kids, enjoyed a monthly "mom's night out," and often talked about faith. God places us next to our physical neighbors on purpose. Get to know them, serve them, cultivate a relationship, and share Jesus with them. However, if they're not open to your faith or turn down your invitations to church or Bible study, keep loving them! Show up in practical ways that reveal the love of Christ in you. They may not be ready to fully explore Christianity, but your good deeds could lower their defenses and help prepare them for a future season when they *are* ready to explore it. You never know; your love, support, laughter, and friendship could be the very thing God uses to redeem their view of Christians.

Community

God placed you in your community on purpose. Think about the struggles in your neighborhood, zip code, or city. Where can you step in and serve others in the name of Jesus? Is there a large homeless population? You could help at the local soup kitchen or pack bags filled with food and an encouraging note to deliver on the street corners. Is there a significant immigrant population? You could volunteer to help a group of women learn English or job skills. Is there a need at your child's school? You could hop on a committee. Are you a seasoned military spouse at a training base for new service members? Be intentional about mentoring newly married military wives. (As we discussed in another chapter, you can't say yes to everything, so don't let these ideas overwhelm you. The goal is simply to identify a need in your community and take a baby step toward it, if you can.)

Work

Your workplace is an excellent opportunity to share the gospel. My Christian neighbor recently told me that his Fort Liberty coworkers frequently ask why he's so happy. The joy he exudes due to his love for God gives him a natural opportunity to share the gospel with others.

As you interact with the people at your job, share your testimony, offer to help others, tell them about the faith-based books you are reading or what God is teaching you in your Bible reading, encourage your coworkers, forgive quickly, and offer grace. They will notice there is something different about you.

Family

If you're anything like me, it's easy to lose sight of your most immediate discipleship opportunity—your family. I tend to look out and see who I can help *out there*, other military spouses, neighbors, church members, or women experiencing a crisis pregnancy. Although there's nothing wrong with looking out, I encourage you to look *in* first.

Focus on the people God has placed within your home. How are you discipling your kids and helping your husband grow in faith? Deuteronomy 6:7 tells us to talk about God with our children throughout the day, regardless of the activity. We can talk about Him while we gaze at the beauty of a flower He created, God's creativity in making an animal you're marveling at, or while encouraging a talent He's given your child while they work on an art project. And as we looked at before, women were created as equal partners to help our husbands; support them in their transformation to become more like Jesus.

Help your family embrace their unique gifts and community to complete the missional work of Christ. For example, if you enjoy being with other people's children, consider serving in the kid's ministry at your church. If your daughter enjoys cooking, she can bring meals to the elderly or another family whose service member is deployed. If your spouse is into physical fitness, he can lead a class in your garage or offer one on your installation.

Consider your family's gifts, talents, and interests, and let these guide you into a potential missional field you can explore.

Chosen

I don't need to tell you this military life is one of deep and regular sacrifice. We sacrifice our professions, friendships, comfort, and stability. We endure deployments, moves, and solo parenting.

According to the Military Spouse Chamber of Commerce, there are nearly one million military spouses of currently serving Active Duty, Guard, and Reserve service members.[2] And to date, the world has 7.8 billion people. That means military spouses are 0.0128 percent of the population. Therefore, God finely selected you to hold this role.

Have you ever viewed your sacrifice as a military spouse as an honor? Of all the people in the world, God chose 0.0128 percent of us to help our service members defend the nation and spread the gospel to our nation's armed forces families. *Your role as a military spouse is not coincidence,* my friend. God wants *you* to be a part of His plan to share the good news of Jesus Christ. Your sacrifice is crucial to bringing others in our community to the feet of Jesus.

Called

The Scriptures are full of real people God called to leave their families, friends, and communities to lead others to Him and spread the gospel. You are not alone.

In Genesis 12, God calls Abram (Abraham) to leave his country, people, and home to go to a foreign land, which would be for his benefit and the benefit of all people (vv. 1–3). I love the statement in verse 4: "So Abram went, as the LORD had told him."

When I first started traveling around the country as a military spouse, I viewed it as exactly that—traveling. I didn't recognize God was *sending* me. In my mind, the men and women over at HRC (Human Resources Command) decided our fate. Now, maturing in my faith and fifteen years into this military life, it feels drastically different.

We're preparing for new orders as I write this. For months, we've been praying for God to close all other doors where He doesn't want us and for us only to be where He needs us (even if we don't want to go there). We're praying for our hearts to be content with His will, knowing He is purposefully sending us where He needs us. That's significantly different from my previous (non-God-honoring) responses to *His* orders that called me to leave.

God also called Jonah to leave his home to share His Word with the wicked people of Ninevah. If you know this popular story, you know that Jonah didn't want to go; he refused God's plan. Thankfully, God rescued Jonah from his defiance. When Jonah finally left to go to Ninevah and share God's message, the whole city of Ninevah repented and believed! No matter how many times we move as military spouses, God doesn't send us anywhere by accident. He plans to use you for His eternal purposes. Wherever you are sent, there are people that need to hear about God, and you're the one called to tell them.

In the New Testament, God calls Paul to leave his home, traveling the world as His chosen instrument, proclaiming the Lord's name. Paul's commitment to God's call was sacrificial. He was shipwrecked, imprisoned, hungry, and persecuted. Our call to proclaim the gospel also requires sacrifice. However, I pray we go out into the world emboldened, knowing we are God's *chosen* instrument. What a gift to be selected by God.

As a chosen instrument of God, the Lord places you where He wants you. When you said, "I do," God orchestrated all the minute details that led you and your husband to that moment. He chose a military man for you because He has plans not just for your husband but for *you* and *your* gifts wherever He takes you. Like Abraham, Jonah, and Paul, will you leave to advance God's kingdom?

If you have orders to Guam, God determined that. If you live in Italy, God sent you there. If you're stationed at Fort Johnson (formerly Fort Polk), God did the stationing. If you're a National Guard family, isolated from the military community, God's own hand guided you there. Wherever you are, that is your mission field.

So, how do we practically live out the truth that the Lord has called us to live, work, serve, and play among the military to spread the good news of Jesus Christ? You may feel intimidated to share the gospel. (I do, too, sometimes! Writing this without looking at your face feels much more comfortable.) Yet we can trust God to equip us in this endeavor. However, we cannot expect to grow in our ability to share the gospel if we don't do the work. Below is a list of ways to begin to pursue a life that rejoices in sharing the truth of Jesus Christ.

1. Identify your spiritual gifts and talents. God has equipped all believers with at least one spiritual gift that we can use to help others experience the love of Jesus, which we see in 1 Peter 4:10: "Just as each one has received a gift, use it to serve others, as good stewards of the varied grace of God."

2. Share your testimony. When you tell others your testimony, it simply means sharing a story of how God has worked in your life. It could be the story about how you came to believe in Christ or an example of a time when God showed Himself as faithful in your life. For instance, my salvation testimony includes coming to believe in Jesus while reading a passage in Max Lucado's book, *3:16: The Numbers of Hope*. One story of how God showed up in my life is when He surrounded me with loving friends who provided meals and babysitting when I miscarried our child.

3. Spend time in God's Word. God gave us the Bible so that we have the gift of knowing Him. If we want to communicate who He is and what He has done for us, reading the book that tells us all we need to know is imperative.

4. Study the Bible. Beyond a cursory reading of the Scriptures, God wants us to explore and *study* His Word to understand what

He wants to tell us. Consider joining a Bible study at your church, joining a study online, purchasing a study Bible, and reading books and websites that teach you how to study God's Word.

5. Enroll in a discipleship class at your local church or online. These classes are designed to teach you how to share the gospel. The most significant (and relieving!) lesson I took away from my first discipleship class was that *I don't have to know everything to share Jesus with others.* If someone asks a question, it's okay to find the answer and get back to them later.

6. Use a tract or "Romans Road." I've heard of some believers who came to know Jesus when someone shared a tract, a small booklet that explains the good news. This tool is helpful for people who may not feel comfortable sharing Jesus verbally or want a simple visual to share the gospel. Romans Road includes six verses from the book of Romans that share the plan of salvation. You can hand these printed verses to someone or, better yet, memorize the six verses to share with others.

7. Study apologetics. In 1 Peter 3:15–16, we see God's call to be equipped with knowledge about Him and His Word: "But in your hearts regard Christ the Lord as holy,

ready at any time to give a defense to anyone who asks you for a reason for the hope that is in you. Yet do this with gentleness and reverence." Apologetics is the defense of the Christian faith with reasoned arguments. There are a plethora of podcasts, books, websites, and videos to help you learn how to defend your faith.

8. Lead a Bible study. This is a great way to share the good news with others. If God has given you the desire to teach, you can lead a study in your home or church.

9. Attend your local PWOC chapter. Protestant Women of the Chapel is a Christian group that meets weekly to worship God, share testimonies of faith, teach the Bible, and fellowship. PWOC currently meets on 137 military installations.

10. Use "The Story" app by Spread Truth Ministries, downloadable to your phone, to share the gospel with someone. This app tells the greater story of the Bible in four acts (*Creation, Fall, Rescue,* and *Restoration*) and how Jesus's saving work factors into the story—all in just a few minutes!

11. Invite a non-Christian to start reading the Bible with you so that you'll be held accountable. An easy way to do this is to simply say, "I want more hope and peace in my daily life, and to get that I've been

wanting to start a Bible reading plan, but
I know I won't keep up with it without a
partner. Would you want to do it with me?"
They will naturally start asking questions as
the two of you keep up your reading plan,
and you can begin spiritual conversations
that eventually lead to the gospel. (An easy
way to do this is through *The Bible Recap* by
Tara-Leigh Cobble.)

Modeling Jesus: A Traveler Who Shared the Gospel

How old were you when you became a military wife? I was
twenty-four. Jesus was about thirty years old when he began his
ministry (Luke 3:23). In his three years of ministry before his
death on the cross, Jesus visited a plethora of towns. Can't we
relate to that?

In each place Jesus visited during his years of ministry, He
shared God's love. He showed people that He was the Messiah.
Regardless of Jesus's uncomfortable, nomadic lifestyle, He
expressed the love and truth of God with others as He shared
meals, served, healed, and taught. We see this modeled in Mark
2:15–17.

> While he was reclining at the table in Levi's
> house, many tax collectors and sinners were
> eating with Jesus and his disciples, for there
> were many who were following him. When the
> scribes who were Pharisees saw that he was eat-
> ing with sinners and tax collectors, they asked

his disciples, "Why does he eat with tax collectors and sinners?"

When Jesus heard this, he told them, "It is not those who are well who need a doctor, but those who are sick. I didn't come to call the righteous, but sinners."

Before verse 15, Jesus calls Levi (soon to be known as Matthew) to follow Him and become one of His disciples. Levi responds immediately, and later that night, Levi hosts a dinner at his house for Jesus, His disciples, and others in the community. Sharing a meal with someone is a beautiful opportunity to begin a relationship, learn another's story, and share your own. Jesus didn't separate from those who didn't believe in Him; He did the opposite. He engaged.

Jesus is our model for fulfilling our calling to share the gospel in love, even while traveling often. Jesus did this in a multitude of ways, and we can too. He recited the Scriptures. He helped. He loved. He spoke the truth. He served. He healed. He listened. He interacted. And He allowed women to sit at His feet while He taught (the posture that a religious teacher's disciple or student would take), something completely countercultural during the time Jesus lived (Luke 10:39). Will we serve those God puts in our lives? Will we draw near to those everyone else would expect us to avoid? Will we dedicate ourselves to God's Word? To sharing it? To teach it to others in our military community?

Warning

Please don't waste your life. Don't fall into the trap of living your life as a fan of Jesus and not a follower. Don't spend all your time resenting where you are and your husband's profession. God has put you there to fulfill your calling, your purpose. The military may cut your orders, but God determines our boundaries and dwelling places.

Therefore, wives should feel *empowered*, knowing their role in this lifestyle is *equally essential* to that of their husbands, from working in their professions, to raising their children, to forging new friendships, to using their gifts in local churches, to serving in their community, to fostering their marriages, to orchestrating moves.

--- *Prayer* ---

Dear Heavenly Father,

You are omniscient, knowing everything there is to know, something I cannot do. And You promise to work everything for my good, even when I can't understand Your higher ways. Please help me trust You and Your wisdom. Lord, thank You for entrusting me with the rare responsibility to share the good news with the military community. This is a selective role, and I want to partner with You to fulfill my duties here. Thank You for sending the Holy Spirit to guide me. Please help me constantly refocus my attention to notice the Spirit's leading—whom to share with, what to say, when to speak, and when to remain quiet. Help me believe that You placed my husband and me within the military on purpose, dissolving any morsels (or epic icebergs) of resentment along the way. Lord, please forgive me for all the times I wished for an easier, different lifestyle, grumbling about where You placed me. Create joy, peace, hope, and love in me as I accept and fulfill the calling to share the gospel with those You bring into my sphere of influence. In Jesus's mighty name, amen.

—————————— *Reflection Questions* ——————————

1. Have you previously been searching for or confused about your purpose in life?

2. Have you ever thought of yourself as a military missionary? Is that knowledge relieving, empowering, confusing, or something else? Why?

3. Share the concept of being a military missionary with your husband, parents, children, and best friends. Return here and record their comments. Were they supportive?

4. What spheres of influence are most natural for you to view as a mission field right now? How might you enter into those spaces with more intentionality this week, this month, or this year?

5. How close does your life currently align with living out a missional military lifestyle (sharing the gospel with those in the military community)?

0	1	2	3	4	5	6	7	8	9	10

Not sharing the gospel   I share on occasion   I can't stop talking about God

6. Now move the marker to where you want to be in twelve months.

0	1	2	3	4	5	6	7	8	9	10

Not sharing the gospel   I share on occasion   I can't stop talking about God

7. What steps do you need to make to advance to where you want to be on the scale?

──────────── *Next Steps* ────────────

❏ Complete a free spiritual gifts test to learn how God uniquely designed you to serve others in the name of Jesus.
❏ Enroll in a discipleship class.
❏ Research the "Romans Road" and memorize the corresponding Scripture verses.
❏ Complete a free spiritual formation course from Practicing the Way.

──────────── *Resources* ────────────

For links and descriptions of each resource, visit Ashleyashcraft.com/missionreadymarriage.

- Cru Military
- NavsMilitary
- Protestant Women of the Chapel
- Lifeway's Spiritual Gifts Assessment
- *Faithfully Different* by Natasha Craine
- *Don't Hold Back* by David Platt
- *Not a Fan* by Kyle Idleman
- *I Don't Have Enough Faith to be an Atheist* by Norman Geisler and Frank Turek

- *Out of the Saltshaker and into the World* by Becky Pippert
- *Stand to Reason* podcast
- *Theology Mom* podcast
- *The Alisa Childers* podcast
- *The Natasha Craine* podcast
- *Journeywomen* podcast
- *Knowing Faith* podcast
- *Red Pen Logic* on YouTube
- *Jesus Revolution*, the film

Chapter Eight

Financial Health: Honoring God with Your Money

I struggle to _____ when
it comes to my finances.

At eighteen years old, I received my first credit card. Throughout college, I bought what I wanted and enjoyed personal loans I never had to repay. By age twenty-three, I bought a car I couldn't pay in full. Saving? Tithing? Investing? Only buying what I could afford? What are those?! Despite my generally responsible nature, I wasn't responsible with my finances.

When Tim and I became engaged, we had a combined total of $120,000 in debt! Between my government-aided student loan, Tim's student loan, our new cars, and our credit card debt, we did not enter marriage in a place of financial health. The amount seemed insurmountable. But God.

During a church service at our sweet Enterprise, Alabama, chapel, an advertisement for Dave Ramsey's Financial Peace University class appeared on the screen. Knowing the statistics for divorce around money issues, I knew we needed to enroll. So, for the next thirteen weeks, we fully invested our time, energy, and resources into learning and following the biblical money principles presented in this program.

Through our hard work in partnering with God, we were able to pay off all our debt in under two years! We budgeted, only lived on Tim's income (reserving all my salary to pay off debt and save), and spent frugally. There were plenty of exciting adventures we missed out on during our first couple of years of marriage. Still, we were more excited by the opportunity to set up our union for financial success—a little sacrifice for a lifetime of wise stewardship of God's money.

Snapshot on Military Finances

Blue Star Families conducted its twelfth annual Military Family Lifestyle Survey in 2021. Capturing the experiences of more than eight thousand respondents worldwide and generating millions of data points, it remains the largest and most comprehensive survey of active-duty, National Guard, reserve service members, veterans, and their families. Here are the latest results that relate to finances as of the writing of this book:

- The top three contributors to financial stress are spouse un/underemployment (41%), student loans (30%), and out-of-pocket relocation expenses (29%).
- Of active-duty families' respondents with student debt, 55 percent owe more than $25,000.

- Military pay was the top concern for 24 percent of respondents.
- Spouse employment was the top concern for 43 percent of respondents.
- Military spouses face unemployment rates that are four times the national average.
- One in three active-duty spouses who are not working cite childcare expenses as the reason.
- Two-thirds (66%) of active-duty family respondents report having unreimbursed out-of-pocket expenses related to their last PCS move, and among those with unreimbursed moving costs, more than half (55%) report those expenses to be over $1,000.[1]

It's Not Your Money

Have you ever thought about the fact that the money in your bank account isn't actually yours? That was shocking news to me as a new Christian at age twenty-three. *I work for my money; I choose how to spend it.* But the Lord was softening my heart and opening my eyes to the truth. Psalm 24:1 tells us, "The earth and everything in it, the world and its inhabitants, belong to the LORD."

"Everything in it" includes money! Because God has graciously given us the freedom of choice, He *allows* us to steward *His* money. So, to succeed with "our finances," we must follow the Creator's principles for handling money.

Thankfully, God doesn't leave us guessing how to steward our finances; the Scriptures boast about twenty-five hundred verses on money. We simply have to make the time to learn what He says and then follow God's directions. While it can be easy to resist the wisdom of the Bible in this area of life, if you courageously push past your resistance and trust God's way of doing money, you'll find out exactly what I found: all of the Lord's financial guidelines are for your good.

Tithing

Tithing is when followers of Christ give 10 percent (or more) of their income to their local church. This can feel scary! You may believe you need that 10 percent to make ends meet, but there are usually plenty of areas where you can cut back on spending to be able to tithe, such as packing lunch at home instead of eating out, cutting down on your entertainment expenses, or eliminating some of your monthly subscription services.

Check out these verses on tithing:

> Honor the LORD with your possessions and with the first produce of your entire harvest; then your barns will be completely filled, and your vats will overflow with new wine. (Prov. 3:9–10)

> Every tenth of the land's produce, grain from the soil or fruit from the trees, belongs to the LORD; it is holy to the LORD. (Lev. 27:30)

"Bring the full tenth into the storehouse so that
there may be food in my house. Test me in this
way," says the LORD of Armies. "See if I will not
open the floodgates of heaven and pour out a
blessing for you without measure." (Mal. 3:10)

These verses may sound foreign because we no longer live
in an agrarian culture (which depended on cultivating the land)
like they did in biblical times. In our modern culture, instead
of offering God 10 percent of our crops, we are to offer God 10
percent of our income, regardless of our occupation.

Do you have to tithe to follow Jesus? No. He loves you, and
your salvation is secured regardless of giving to your local church.
But sadly, the Christian Stewardship Network reports that only
10–15 percent of Christians tithe.[2] That's a shockingly low number. My question then is this: What blessings are 85–90 percent
of Christians missing out on because they're not entrusting their
"firstfruits" to God?

You may be wondering if you should tithe when you are in
debt. Ramsey Solutions recommends that even those in debt
should tithe because you can still exhibit a posture of generosity while you're paying off debt. It's all about trusting God with
your money.

Finally, what do you do about tithing after you move to a
new location and before you've found a new church home? Tim
and I continue to tithe to our previous church until we've iden-
tified the new church we'll regularly attend. When planning a
move, pray and seek God's guidance on this issue.

A final word on tithing and giving that has taken me time
to realize: the virtue of generosity isn't something that will

magically pop up in your character later down the line. Whatever you are doing today is forming a habit for the person you'll be in the future. If you've got excuses for not being generous now, by the time "later" comes, you won't be a generous person. Rather, you'll be a person who *wanted* to be generous way back when but never got around to it. Why? Because the habit you built was to keep your tithe over and over again instead of giving it away. Who you are tomorrow will be either a person conditioned to give your first and best to God's kingdom or a person conditioned to hold these things back from Him. In short, who we are tomorrow is formed not by our intentions—good as they may be—but by the habits we start today.

You're Already Free; Don't Be a Slave Again

God has a history of saving His people. He rescued the Israelites from Egyptian slavery. He brought them out of the desert into the promised land of Canaan. He used a young Jewish queen to save the Israelites from Babylonian annihilation. And He brought His one and only Son into our world as a baby to defeat sin and death, rescuing those who believe in Jesus from an eternity without Him.

And despite all God's rescue missions, His people tend to fall back into captivity. I tend to fall back into captivity. You tend to fall back into captivity. Why is that? Because on the inside, we're a house divided. While the Spirit in us desires to honor God and walk in His ways, the "flesh" in us (the sinful part of our nature) works against the Spirit and tempts us to be greedy, discontent, and indulgent. This is especially true with our finances. (In fact, 76 percent of military families and veterans carry debt.[3])

Galatians 5:17 (NASB) explains it this way: "The desire of the flesh is against the Spirit, and the Spirit against the flesh; for these are in opposition to one another, in order to keep you from doing whatever you want."

Do you ever feel this war within? Like one part of you wants to honor God with your money (and all other areas of life), but another part of you doesn't? Like your deepest desire is to follow Jesus faithfully, but there's something working against this desire, tempting you away from it? That's the Holy Spirit and the flesh going to war with each other inside of you! And you're not alone in this war. Even the apostle Paul—a writer of Scripture and the world's most famous church planter—felt this classic struggle within himself too:

> So the trouble is not with the law, for it is spiritual and good. The trouble is with me, for I am all too human, a slave to sin. I don't really understand myself, for I want to do what is right, but I don't do it. Instead, I do what I hate. But if I know that what I am doing is wrong, this shows that I agree that the law is good. So I am not the one doing wrong; it is sin living in me that does it.
>
> And I know that nothing good lives in me, that is, in my sinful nature. I want to do what is right, but I can't. I want to do what is good, but I don't. I don't want to do what is wrong, but I do it anyway. But if I do what I don't want to do, I am not really the one doing wrong; it is sin living in me that does it.

> I have discovered this principle of life—that
> when I want to do right, evil lies close at hand.
> I love God's law with all my heart. But there is
> another power within me that is at war with my
> mind. This power makes me a slave to the sin
> that is still within me. Oh, what a miserable per-
> son I am! Who will free me from this life that
> is dominated by sin and death? Thank God!
> The answer is in Jesus Christ our Lord. (Rom.
> 7:14–21a [NLT], 21b [ESV], 22–25a [NLT])

Here's the good news in the battle between the Spirit and the flesh: even when your sinful nature rears its ugly head, the Holy Spirit inside of you is stronger and has the power to defeat any temptation you feel. Why? Because the Holy Spirit is God! And God is stronger than any struggle. With the Spirit in you, you have all the power you need to overcome the pull of your flesh when it comes to money or any other battle. You don't have to be a slave to your flesh; you *can* walk in victory and freedom and obedience to God, even when it's hard. Paul puts it this way: "I say, then, walk by the Spirit and you will certainly not carry out the desire of the flesh" (Gal. 5:16).

Common Money Stressors in the Military

One way your flesh can flare up more than usual is when you're being *re*active to financial stressors instead of *pro*active. When you consider certain stressors before they pop up, you're more likely to handle them in God-honoring ways and avoid debt. Here are some of those stressors.

Moving

Military members typically move every one to three years, and some families move more than once yearly. With each new set of orders comes a plethora of expenses, some of which never get reimbursed. Consider adding a savings account designated for future moves so you don't have to go into debt with each move.

Deployment and Training

Besides the stress of separation from our service members, we incur added expenses when our husbands are away on duty. We may have to pay for childcare when our spouse would typically watch the kids or for a repair job that our husbands would perform on the cars or house. Think of people in your circle of friends, community, or church whom you can trust to provide these services in your husband's absence, possibly for free.

Additionally, there will likely be times when military spouses have to make difficult financial decisions alone if their service member is away on duty and unable to communicate. When Tim was deployed to Afghanistan, I bought a tiny white Maltese/Yorkie from a local shelter in Texas. That inexpensive $20 dog turned into a $2,000 veterinarian visit when I learned she was severely ill. What would your spouse want you to do in that situation? Sometimes we don't know and have to make a tough call. But we can try our best to plan ahead by discussing spending goals and emergency expenditure plans before any separations.

Housing

With the limited availability of housing on military installations and the rising cost of renting and home ownership, housing costs can be a struggle for some military families. Depending on the market, try to find a property with monthly payments that fall *below* your allotment for housing.

Medical Expenses

Although military families are offered free health care under the basic plan, some families choose to enroll in the military's alternate health insurance plan, which offers more choices for providers but comes with a cost. At some military installations, there are not enough providers and, therefore, not enough appointments to properly treat their patients, forcing some families to use urgent care in place of primary doctors. Other times, military health-care insurance will not pay for the doctors needed for medically complex family members. In those cases, paying for each medical appointment outside of free coverage becomes necessary. Also, many of these specialized appointments require travel expenses and specialized testing or procedures, which insurance may not reimburse. If something like this comes up in your family, try to obtain a good faith estimate of the charges from multiple medical providers. That way you can compare costs and go with whichever one is most affordable for your situation. You can also ask for financial aid application or a special discount.

Finally, your spouse may be eligible for temporary duty and the associated per diem if one of your family members requires extended medical care away from home. If you're ever in this situation, have your spouse reference both the Federal Travel Regulation and the Joint Travel Regulation for possible benefits. Additionally, if you're referred by your primary care manager for a medical need that is more than one hundred miles away, you may be able to receive financial benefits from your military health-care plan. If housing is required, Fisher House offers free lodging for military and veteran families when a loved one is in the hospital. If a Fisher House is not located near your medical facility, you may be eligible for one of their other programs, Hotels for Heroes. They also have a program for plane tickets called Hero Miles. When our daughter was born with multiple heart defects at a hospital seventy-five miles away from our home, we used the Hotels for Heros program until our room at the Ronald McDonald House was ready. There really are a host of supportive options for military families; we just have to know about them!

Traveling Home

Most military families are stationed away from their families, which often requires significant financial investment to travel home for visits, holidays, and emergencies. Some expenses include plane tickets, airport parking, baggage fees, gas, hotels, car rentals, food, and house and pet sitters. The stress around this significantly decreases if you and your spouse discuss how many times a year you plan to go home instead of just winging it and hoping the finances can support extra, unplanned trips.

Food

According to the U.S. Department of Defense, 24 percent of active-duty military members battle with food insecurity, with junior enlisted personnel being the most affected.[4] Grocery prices have skyrocketed recently, causing significant financial stress for many military families. Many installations have resources to help alleviate this issue, including food pantries and free educational classes.

Student Loans

Many military families are burdened by student loans after graduation. This debt often takes years to pay off. Consider enrolling in a financial course or seeking advice from a financial advisor to help. The military offers free financial advisors to assist service members and their families.

Spouse Unemployment or Underemployment

As you read earlier in the chapter, military spouse unemployment rates are four times the national average, causing financial stress for families that need additional income. Also, childcare off base is often too expensive, while childcare on base is usually full, further complicating the issue. Thankfully, there are a host of companies and organizations available to help military spouses find adequate employment.

Spender or Saver?

When Tim and I took the Financial Peace University course, we had to identify ourselves as the "spender" or the "saver" in the relationship. Because God often places us with people who tend to be our opposite (to refine us more into Christ's image), you and your husband likely tend to handle money differently, which causes conflict.

Conflict with money affects a majority of couples. The Center for Faith and Culture states that ". . . money appears to be crushing our marriages." The article continues to explain that "70 percent of couples argue about money, and 57 percent of divorced couples point to arguments about money as the reasons for their divorce."[5]

If you are the "saver" in your marriage, you value security, savings, stability, and wise spending habits. You take time to consider a large purchase. You only buy something on your list to pick up at the store. You save or invest your money immediately upon receiving it. You wait for holidays to purchase expensive items to get them on sale. Conversely, you likely frustrate your spouse because you don't want to spend your money on things or experiences that don't seem necessary.

As the spender, you may value decorating your home, having a diverse wardrobe, vacations, and spontaneous spending on activities. You use your money to invest in the people you love, the place you live, and the experiences that bring you together. Spenders often frustrate their spouses because they tend to be impulsive with their purchases, spend new income quickly, justify spending based on sales, buy items not on their shopping list or allotted in the monthly budget, and view spontaneous purchases as fun.

If your spouse handles money differently from you, remember that your spouse is not the enemy. It is okay to be either a spender or a saver, but we do have to learn to be wise with the way God designed us. The big goals are to keep the lines of communication open with our spouses and come up with an agreement that makes reasonable space and "wins" for both personalities.

The Seven Baby Steps to Financial Freedom

So, how do we wisely handle the money God has given us to manage? Based on experience, I know the seven steps proposed by Dave Ramsey work. But it's not just about paying off debt and learning to save. The ultimate goal is to leave a legacy for your loved ones and to achieve a financial status that allows you to give generously.

Ramsey's website introduces his seven-step program this way: "Dave Ramsey's 7 Baby Steps will show you how to save for emergencies, pay off all your debt for good, and build wealth. It's not a fairy tale. It works every single time!" So let's take a brief look at the seven steps that lead to financial freedom.

> Step 1: Save $1,000 for your starter emergency fund.
>
> Step 2: Pay off all debt (except the house) using the debt snowball.
>
> Step 3: Save three to six months of expenses in a fully funded emergency fund.
>
> Step 4: Invest 15 percent of your household income in retirement.
>
> Step 5: Save for your children's college fund.
>
> Step 6: Pay off your home early.
>
> Step 7: Build wealth and give.[6]

As grateful as I am to have walked through each of the seven baby steps, the last one is the most exciting and rewarding, giving generously within the community God's placed us. Stepping in to financially assist our brothers and sisters in arms, especially our Gold Star Families, is an immense blessing for which we have FPU to thank!

For further information and specific steps for each category, consider enrolling in Financial Peace University. This course is offered at many local churches, military installations, or online. Active-duty military families receive this program completely free!

Obviously, there are many other financial advisors and plans you can turn to for advice. I'm simply sharing the one that's worked for us (and millions of others).

Keys to Our Financial Success

There's no question that I am the spender in my marriage, and Tim is the saver. I'm quick to pick up a few more items at the store than I anticipated, stop to buy a meal for a homeless person on the corner, purchase an item I don't *need*, grab an unplanned snack at a fast-food restaurant, and give the server a hefty tip. Tim, however, makes regular appointments to talk with our financial planner, checks our investments daily, advocates for a monthly budget, and talks me out of large purchases.

Because we've learned to value our differences and combine our financial strengths as "spender" and "saver" (even though we still frustrate each other!), our marriage is financially secure. And by "financially secure," I don't mean we're millionaires. Instead, we trust each other with our finances because we have agreed-on rules and an understanding of how we handle our money. We're honest and transparent with each other. Here are several "money rules" we live by that allow us to live in financial health and remain united when we've been in straining financial situations (like when we lost all our physical belongings). These items are nonnegotiable.

- Lifelong commitment to living debt free. For years after completing FPU, we did not own a single credit card. We only spent what we had in our checking account. Now that we're disciplined financially, we use credit cards for extra benefits like free hotel nights, airline miles, and cashback rewards. However, we pay off our monthly credit card bill, never leaving a balance.

- The first expenditure we have each month is a tithe to our church. God calls all believers to give 10 percent of their earnings to the church, and He promises to bless us when we do so.

- The next item automatically deducted from our checking account each month is savings. We have a savings account for each of our children's college funds, a car fund (so we can pay for a car in full when needed), a home fund (for a down payment on a future home), retirement accounts for both of us, an emergency fund, and a travel fund.

- Tim and I have agreed to consult each other before making purchases over $100 (outside of groceries, which are always over that each week).

- To have transparency and accountability, we do not have separate bank accounts to which the other does not have access. We share our checking account and all savings and investment accounts.
- We spend less than we make to account for the inevitable unexpected monthly expenses.
- We sit down together each month to create a monthly budget.

Modeling Jesus with Money: Sharing with the Owner

Money matters to Jesus, not for personal gain but because our relationship with money tells the status of our hearts. And God tells us He doesn't care about the outside appearance as we do; He cares about what's in our hearts. Matthew 6:21 says, "For where your treasure is, there your heart will be also." This tells us that how we spend our money reflects what's important to us.

Out of the forty parables Jesus used to teach, eleven of them address money. As I said, it mattered to Him because He cares about us.

One of those parables is known as the parable of the tenants. Before teaching this parable in Luke 20, Jesus entered the temple courts during Passover (the feast that celebrates when God freed His people from Egyptian slavery). When He saw that God's house was being used to monetarily take advantage of His people (one, by selling animals for sacrifice, and two, at an abusive cost), He flipped the tables, outraging the Jewish leaders in charge. Following this dramatic statement about the sanctity of the temple, Jesus used a parable to clarify His point.

> And he began to tell the people this parable: "A man planted a vineyard and let it out to tenants and went into another country for a long while. When the time came, he sent a servant to the tenants, so that they would give him some of the fruit of the vineyard. But the tenants beat him and sent him away empty-handed. And he sent another servant. But they also beat and treated him shamefully, and sent him away empty-handed. And he sent yet a third. This one also they wounded and cast out. Then the owner of the vineyard said, 'What shall I do? I will send my beloved son; perhaps they will respect him.' But when the tenants saw him, they said to them-selves, 'This is the heir. Let us kill him, so that the inheritance may be ours.' And they threw him out of the vineyard and killed him. What then will the owner of the vineyard do to them? He will come and destroy those tenants and give the vineyard to others." When they heard this, they said, "Surely not!" But he looked directly at them and said, "What then is this that is written:
>
> > "'The stone that the builders rejected
> > has become the cornerstone?'

Everyone who falls on that stone will be
broken to pieces, and when it falls on anyone, it
will crush him." (Luke 20:9–18 ESV)

In this parable, the man who plants the vineyard represents
God, the vineyard symbolizes Israel, the tenants are the Jewish
religious leaders, the servants represent prophets (God's messen-
gers), and the beloved son is Jesus. Christ uses this story to expose
the hearts of the religious leaders who desperately seek a valid
reason to arrest and kill Him to protect against any loss of their
power. At the end of the story, we see the death of Jesus predicted
and God's announcement that His "vineyard" would soon be
available to all those who believed in Him (not just the Israelites)
and that all unbelievers would be cast out of His family.

When I study this parable, I immediately see greed, my
greed, our human greed. Even though God is responsible for
gifting us with our financial wealth, we tend to close the gate to
the "vineyard" and keep it all for ourselves. To our sinful flesh,
that feels safer. We need it all! Don't we? Yet the safest place we
can put ourselves is inside the will of God.

To be in the will of God, financially speaking, means to
share our "produce" with the King of kings. Even though we may
work and harvest, He planted. And despite our greedy nature, it's
essential we focus on God's generosity as the landowner of our
lives. He allows us to keep *90 percent* of the harvest—*90 percent*!
Are any of you giving someone else 90 percent of your income?
I'm not! He only asks us to give 10 percent to His church. We
can do this. We're called to do this. (In fact, when we start doing
this faithfully, we actually become people who want to be even
more generous with our entire lives. Participating in tithing can

change you on the heart level!). So let's be obedient and see how He works in return.

Prayer

Dear Heavenly Father,

I praise You for Your undeserved generosity. Your heart is focused on giving: giving life, giving love, giving hope, giving provisions. May I model this aspect of Your character in my life. Help me give to my family, friends, community, military installation, and You. Lord, please guide us in how to manage our finances. Thank You that Your Word is filled with wisdom on how to make wise choices with my money. Help me make the hard choice, but the right choice, to follow Your commands surrounding finances. In Jesus's provisional name, amen.

Reflection Questions

1. What are your most significant financial stressors as a military family?

2. In what ways can you relate to the tenants in Jesus's parable? Where are you selfish with the money God's entrusted you with?

3. What does your bank account statement show is most important to you? Write down the three categories that receive the most money from you (groceries, rent, church, charity, entertainment services, delivery boxes, shopping, etc.).

4. Is tithing a regular part of your financial spending? If so, what blessings have you seen come from giving God your first

10 percent each month? If not, what's holding you back from following God's command to tithe?

5. In the parable of the tenants, to which character do you most relate and why?

Next Steps

- ❏ Enroll in Financial Peace University (free for active-duty families!).
- ❏ Make a budget with your spouse.
- ❏ Assess your debt as a couple and come up with a plan to eliminate it.
- ❏ Discuss tithing with your husband and consider giving 10 percent of your income to your local church.
- ❏ Pray about other ways to give generously with your money.

Resources

For links and descriptions of each resource, visit Ashleyashcraft.com/missionreadymarriage.

- *The Total Money Makeover* by Dave Ramsey
- *Money, Possessions, and Eternity* by Randy Alcorn
- *Master Your Money* by Ron Blue
- *God and Money* by John Cortines and Gregory Baumer

- *Military Stewardship Devotional* by American Bible Society
- *The Money Challenge* by Art Rainer
- *The Marriage Challenge* by Art Rainer
- *The Military Money Manual* by Spencer C. Reese
- *The Rachel Cruz Show* podcast
- *Military Money Manual* podcast
- MilSpouse Money Mission
- MilTax
- DOD Office of Financial Readiness
- Hands on Banking
- Military Spouse scholarship opportunities
- Express Loan Program by Small Business Administration
- GI Bill for College
- VA Home Loan
- First Command Financial
- USAA
- Armed Forces Insurance
- Public Service Loan Forgiveness Program
- The National Defense Student Loan Discharge program
- Military Loan Repayment Programs
- Christian Stewardship Network
- Compass—Finances God's Way
- Christian Credit Counselors
- Crown Financial Ministries

Chapter Nine

Moving: Relocating with Confidence

The hardest part of moving
is _____.

I allow myself an annual "military meltdown." It's only fair, don't you think? After a year filled with my husband's on-and-off absence, an absurd amount of changed plans, my award-winning display of flexibility (we can award ourselves, can't we?), solo parenting, and just making it through the ordinary tribulations of life, my knees eventually give. And it usually shows up right around moving day.

In 2016, a couple of weeks before our move from Alabama to New York, the time felt suitable for one of my meltdowns. Alright, so maybe it wasn't a meltdown. It was more of a slow collapse in defeat. A gesture intended to bring some comical relief while planning our ninth military move.

Since we had a seventeen-month-old and a three-and-a-half-year-old at the time, no real adult conversation occurred between

6:00 a.m. and 9:00 p.m. Then, when there was finally time to talk about serious topics like the move, my husband and I were exhausted, and Tim still had to study to prepare for his coursework the next day. We knew we had to plan our move on Friday night, even if it involved some guesswork.

At 10:00 p.m., we started the conversation. We wrote down six different options for the move, all of which seemed workable and of which had a downside. We kept asking, "Which is the least worst option?" By 11:00 p.m., my brain and emotions were done.

On a walk to the kitchen for some water, I melted to the brown tile flooring to show off my exhaustion over the topic, but I couldn't get up. And then the tears came, and I knew my little show wasn't a little show.

While I was down on the floor, I let myself bask in some sorrow and frustration, and then I decided I needed some God. *Lord, give me the strength to prepare for this next move. Show us what You would have us do to prepare. God, I know You are working in this situation. Please give me Your perspective and help me be thankful for this lifestyle and all You've blessed us with. You are in control.*

Giving the move over to the One in control, I pulled myself off the floor. The tears dried up, and I was ready to return to planning our move with my husband—but not before he comforted me with a pint of salted dark chocolate ice cream! When I sat back down at the table, I expressed my feelings to Tim, and within two minutes of my prayer, we decided on a course of action. Tim explained that he had been praying about our move and felt God leading us in one specific direction.

The Power of Prayer

Moving in confidence begins with prayer. Period. I've done it enough times without specific, strategic prayer to know you can't move well when you don't communicate with the One sending you. Without deep prayer, I've moved filled with resentment and hostility toward my husband and his career. On the other hand, moving well means we go confidently, trusting that God is sending us to our next duty station for His kingdom purposes with our best in mind. Remember Acts 17:26? God determines our boundaries, so when we get orders (whether we like the destination or not), the Lord has a plan for us there.

To move confidently requires the preparation of our hearts. And the Lord is the only One who can do that. In the fall of 2019, my husband partook in the Army's new job marketplace system, similar to matchmaking, where a Soldier marks his first choice for a job at a particular installation, and a unit ranks their first choice to fill an open position. If you get a "one-to-one match," you're almost guaranteed to go to the unit of your choice.

We prayed several times daily as we prepared to rank which units we wanted to go to next. We asked God to guide us in our selections (acknowledging He already knew the outcome). Tim and I prayed that all the doors would be closed where we weren't supposed to be and that only the one we needed to walk through would remain open. That's not an easy prayer when you have reasons you want to be in specific locations or with certain units, but we trust God's faithfulness enough to go with open hands, accepting where He places us.

One afternoon in the spring of 2020, the kids and I walked home from a playdate and were greeted by Tim playing Hawaiian music and dancing the hula. Joy erupted over the new adventure we were about to embark on! After learning he had a "one-to-one match" and receiving an official request for orders, we started preparing for our move to paradise.

However, a few weeks before we were set to move, the Army surprised us and switched our orders to Fort Liberty, North Carolina (which was literally Tim's fifty-second choice!). Because I had spent significant time in prayer and I knew that God was ultimately in charge, I was able to pivot gracefully, something I definitely failed to do earlier in Tim's military career.

Making Preparations

After prayer comes the practical work of preparing to move: coordinating movers, finding a new home, registering the kids for school, applying for a new job, and so on. Although sometimes this can be exciting (like finding a new home you love), most of it is frustrating, annoying, and all-consuming. Below are several ideas to help you prepare to move in confidence.

Budgeting

There's a common perception that the government pays for all your moving expenses. (Did you just laugh out loud at that line? Me too!) If you've moved at least once, you know that's not true. Yes, you get reimbursed for certain expenses up to a specific dollar amount, like gas, hotels, and moving costs. However, you're often left with hundreds, if not thousands, of dollars in out-of-pocket expenses. Thus, it's imperative to create a budget and start saving ahead of time! Make a list of all the items you'll need to purchase and leave a category for unexpected expenses (like curtains because you have more windows in the new house, an extra bedroom you want to furnish, or the hotel that costs more than the government allots).

Home Search

If you plan to live on base, you likely won't have much choice in where you live or when you get to move in, as it's based on availability. However, at some duty stations, you may get to select a house or neighborhood, so check out your options in person or online ahead of time. If you plan to live off post, you'll need to decide if it's wiser financially to buy or rent (consider your income, your savings, how long you'll be at the next installation, and the current housing market).

School Search

Before you move, knowing what school your kids will attend is helpful. However, you may only be able to solidify this once you have secured housing. In addition, if any of your children have special needs, you'll need to find out if your preferred or assigned school can accommodate your child's education plan. Today, several schooling options exist, from DOD (Department of Defense), charter, public, private, religious, homeschool, co-ops, Montessori, and more. You can also check school scores online to see how they are ranked.

Church Search

As discussed earlier, start looking online at the churches in the area you're moving to before you PCS. Most church websites offer the opportunity to listen to their church services online so you can see if you like the preaching ahead of time. Also, look online to see all the programs offered. For example, do they have small groups, Sunday school, kids ministry, youth services, military ministry, and so on? If you know someone who has previously been to your new duty station, ask them for a recommendation. You can also inquire about churches on your new installation's social media spouse page.

PCS Binder

Putting all your moving documents in one binder is extremely helpful. Organizing your paperwork in one place will ensure less stress on both ends of the move. For example, your binder can include a set of your husband's orders; a place to keep all your gas, food, and car weight receipts; a list of schools and churches you're considering; and everything you need to do. My friend Mallory, the creator of DITY Mama, has a free PCS binder download on her website that is immensely helpful. We printed it out and used all her worksheets and suggestions during our last move, and we won't move again without it!

Health Care

Another area you have to cover before you move is health care. Ensure you have a copy of all your documents from health-care providers. Also, sign any medical release forms, if needed. Look for doctors around your new duty station and start making appointments for your first visits now if you have medical issues that require continued or specialty care.

Employment

If you plan to work at your next location, start researching job opportunities in your new area and applying for positions once you receive orders. There are many free websites dedicated to helping military spouses find employment.

Kids

Amid all our planning, it's essential that we remember to include our kids in the planning. DITY Mama also offers a free *kids* PCS packet that I highly recommend. Show your kids their new town on the computer, check out exciting places you can visit together, ask them to help plan adventures along the move route, view pictures of your new house, and pick out updated bedroom decor for their future bedroom (if finances allow).

Leaving Your Current Duty Station

Leaving can be the hardest part of the moving process, or maybe you've been eager to go since you first arrived! If you've established a community of friends, plan to see them all before you leave. Ensure your kids get a chance to say goodbye to their closest friends too. Consider hosting a going-away party to say all your farewells at once, or plan a month in advance to meet up individually with your friends to say goodbye.

In Transit

Despite all the stress that comes with moving, this part has the potential to be fun. Before you move, plan out adventures along the way. Look at a map and decide which towns you will stop in to explore or stay the night. There will likely be exciting attractions, amusement parks, museums, beaches, and hiking trails along your route (even if you have to make a little detour for the historical markers your husband must see). Moving is also an excellent opportunity to catch up with old friends from past duty stations. As we plan our stops, we often realize that friends or family live nearby and use our travels to spend time with loved ones we wouldn't see otherwise.

Settling In

Settling in may be the most challenging part of moving, making your new house feel like home. Between all the unpacking, all the phone calls (utilities, doctors, Internet provider, trash company, schools, etc.), and all the emotions, the idea of feeling settled upon arrival at your new duty station feels like the antithesis of reality. So, how do we make a strange place feel like home?

1. Give yourself and your family members lots of grace. Moving causes significant strain and stress on everyone. Plan for emotions to rise and fall frequently and unexpectedly.
2. Create (or find) community. Friendships are a crucial step in making our new locations feel like home. Whatever you're into, create a group and invite others to join you, or look for an existing local class, group, or club.

3. Go to church. We may be tempted to put this one on the back burner until we feel settled, but I challenge our military community to prioritize attending church soon after a move. You can quickly meet like-minded friends, join groups, and develop a support system.

4. Find a babysitter. It's hard to trust strangers, but find recommendations for a beloved babysitter in your area. After all the stress of moving, going on a date with your husband will be much needed. And make it a regular event!

5. Explore. You may feel like holing up in your new house and getting everything put away, and that's fine, but make time to step away from all the to-dos and explore your new town. Find activities your family will enjoy and embrace the new attractions, culture, and cuisine.

Relocation Depression

When one of my children experienced significant behavioral change after a move, a developmental pediatrician diagnosed my child with transition disorder. At that point, our kid had lived in three homes in twelve months (not including all the hotels!). So if you experience depression, anxiety, or anger after a military move, you are not the only one.

An article from the counseling business BetterHelp states that "millions of people worldwide experience depression, and among those are individuals who are living with temporary relocation depression." The article continues to explain that "relocation depression is a type of situational depression that occurs after relocating or moving. This type of depression is not listed in the DSM-V but may have similar symptoms to clinical depression on a short-term basis. Your symptoms are real, and support is available to you.

If you suffer from relocation depression, you may experience one or more of these symptoms, as listed by BetterHelp:

- Feeling down or experiencing a persistent low mood
- Feelings of anger or irritability
- Appetite changes
- Weight changes
- Changes in sleep schedule
- Loss of interest in regular activities
- Social withdrawal
- Difficulty completing daily tasks
- Difficulty with personal or sleep hygiene
- Thoughts of suicide[1]

If you are currently experiencing symptoms of relocation depression after moving, or if it happens in the future, please seek help from your doctor and a counselor to assist you in moving toward healing. You are not alone!

Dissatisfaction

What if you don't like the new duty station you're headed to or where you're currently located? Trust me, I understand. As we drove into El Paso, Texas, for the first time, our cars packed with our most needed belongings until the moving truck arrived, the skies were aswirl with dust. As we viewed our new home from the freeway, the city was masked in beige sand. It was barren, barren, barren, and I ached for the lush emerald trees of Alabama we'd left behind. Sadly, my feelings never changed toward El Paso. Sure, we found a few restaurants we liked, a church home, and made some friends, but my attitude about the "boring brown town" kept me from embracing all God had for me there.

Please hear me say it's absolutely permissible to feel a deep sense of grief and frustration; just read the Psalms for confirmation. But, like with the psalmists, we can't stay there. After allowing ourselves to feel all the emotions, we need to return our thoughts to the goodness of God and praise Him for where He's intentionally placed us.

When you're ready, adventure across your city, explore all it has to offer, find the hidden gems and the best local cuisine, invite people into your home and build lasting friendships, find a church and invest in serving there, and listen for where God is directing you to spend your time. Make it feel like your hometown instead of just another duty station along the way. That's how we move into satisfaction. Embrace the blessings He has for you wherever He sends you! After all, evidences of His grace are tucked into all sorts of nooks and crannies across the globe. Even in El Paso.

Modeling Jesus: Following Your Purpose

As we've already discovered, our purpose as believers in Christ is to love others and spread the good news of Jesus— making disciples, baptizing them, and teaching them to obey all of God's commands (Matt. 28:19–20). God gives believers different places and people groups to accomplish this worldwide task. As military wives, God chose for us to speak truth into the armed services community.

In Luke 4:42–44 (ESV), we see Jesus obeying God's call for him to travel to the "other towns," preaching the truth of the gospel.

> And when it was day, he departed and went into a desolate place. And the people sought him and came to him, and would have kept him from leaving them, but he said to them, "I must preach the good news of the kingdom of God to the other towns as well; for I was sent for this purpose." And he was preaching in the synagogues of Judea.

Before this passage, the Scriptures tell us that Jesus spent the previous day healing all those who were sick with various diseases, and "he laid his hands on every one of them and healed them" (v. 40 ESV). I want you to notice that after doing the Lord's work of healing and serving the community, Jesus went away by himself to pray.

One of the reasons He did this was to listen to God's plan. After spending time with the Father, He knew. His heart was oriented and obedient. Even though the people wanted the Messiah to stay, Jesus knew from His alone time with God that the Lord wanted Him to move on to other towns.

As military wives, modeling Jesus's time in prayer and obedience to the Father will serve us exponentially. If we spend time talking to God and listening to His will, we'll be prepared to help others wherever He may send us. And our hearts will align themselves with God's will in the process. As much as moving on was God's plan for Jesus, it's also the Lord's plan for us. Say this verse aloud, inserting your name in the blank space: "I, _____, must preach the good news of the kingdom of God to the other towns as well; for I was sent for this purpose."

Prayer

Dear Heavenly Father,

You ultimately choose the locations the military sends my family and me. I'm thankful that I can trust Your decision regarding my boundaries. Please remind me to pray, seek Your will, and align my heart to Yours as I prepare for future moves. Lord, when the orders come, please help me be content with the next mission field You've placed in my path. As I pack up and leave behind all my comforts and friendships, fill me with Your unexplainable peace. Guide me in being a godly example to my family of what it looks like to trust You with a joyful heart. Please help me give my family and myself grace in the transition and aid us in seeking appropriate health care if depression or anxiety arises. Lord, You chose a transitionary lifestyle for me. Show me how to model Jesus as I move from town to town, and help me proclaim Your Word boldly to all You place in my sphere of influence. In Jesus's wise name, amen.

Reflection Questions

1. Do you allow yourself the freedom to have a "military meltdown" occasionally? Why or why not?

2. In your past military moves, which move was the most difficult? Why?

3. Is prayer a regular part of your moving preparation? If not, how can you incorporate it into your moving to-do list?

4. Which part of the planning process is the most challenging for you regarding moving? Can any ideas in this chapter better prepare you next time?

5. Name an aspect of moving that you like.

6. Have you ever experienced a form of relocation depression? If so, did you seek help? Why or why not?

Next Steps

❑ Create a budget for your next move.
❑ Organize a PCS binder.
❑ Print out a moving packet for your kids.
❑ Before a PCS, ask your new unit if they have a sponsor program that assists incoming families with their move.
❑ Pray for God to prepare your heart for your next duty station.

Resources

For links and descriptions of each resource, visit
Ashleyashcraft.com/missionreadymarriage.

- *After the Boxes Are Unpacked: Moving on After Moving In* by Susan Miller
- *But Mom, I Don't Want to Move: Easing the Impact of Moving on Your Children* by Susan Miller
- *Another Move, God?* by Beth Runkle
- *Flourish: Wherever the Military Sends You* by Planting Roots
- *Directed* by Brenda Pace
- *PCS with Military.com* podcast
- DITY Mama
- Military OneSource
- MILLIE
- PCS Like a Pro
- MyPCS
- My Ultimate PCS app
- PCS Grades

Chapter Ten

Parenting Military Style: Trusting God's Plan for Our Kids

Because my children are growing
up in the military, I worry
that _____.

"Hi, this is Caroline from Pinehurst Surgical Center calling for Ashley Ashcraft. We received the gender result from your blood test, so please call me back to review the findings." When I dialed the doctor's office, I planned to ask the nurse to write down our baby's gender on a card and leave it in an envelope at the front desk.

Gender reveal parties weren't a thing when I was pregnant with our first three children, and Tim wanted to shoot off some colored confetti this time. (By the way, the day after we shot off five confetti poppers in the backyard, filled with *thousands* of tiny pieces of paper, guess who had to clean it up alone because her husband left for field training for a week!) But instead of hanging up after I made my request, the nurse said she needed to tell me something that came back from my blood sampling.

"Due to your mature age, there is a one out of eighty-six chance your baby can have Down syndrome. However, your blood results show that there is a nine out of ten chance your baby has Down syndrome. You need to make an appointment with a genetic counselor to review the findings, and we will refer you to see a high-risk doctor at Duke."

Holding it together, I asked a few questions about this unexpected revelation and then hung up. Next, I texted my husband (who is always in a meeting with someone) that I needed him to call me immediately. He called right away, and I couldn't do more than cry. Then, finally, the nurse's words reverberated from my vocal cords. Tim rushed home to comfort me—something you know our service members can't readily do.

As I waited for Tim to arrive home, I knew I needed to be with God and cling to the truth in His Word. Since the beginning of my pregnancy, I'd been praying Psalm 139 and Luke 1:46–55 over our baby. Before I opened those pages, I wrote down some of my fears: people might judge me for having a baby at this age; the baby may have serious medical complications; my life will be different than I planned; I can't handle another child with special needs.

Then I turned to the passages I'd been praying over our baby and wrote down the character traits of God and His promises held within those sacred pages: God is intricately weaving my baby; He speaks to His people and offers mercy; He knows the number of days my child will live before one comes to pass. Reminding myself of His love and omniscience helped calm the fears that tried to deceive me.

As military wives, we will inevitably face parenting challenges that shock, scare, and tempt us to feel guilt and shame. We'll feel alone, stranded, and question our abilities. We'll battle fatigue and the desire to give up as we solo parent and deal with our children's emotions and behaviors. However, if we learn to turn to Scripture in those moments and remind ourselves of who our good God is, we can continue persevering and trusting His plan for our lives and those of our kids.

Whatever parenting struggle leaves us riddled with anxiety, whether it's related to the military or not, our children's Creator is the ultimate source of strength and hope.

Side note: I submitted the manuscript for this book while living in the Ronald McDonald House when our baby was in the NICU. Finley was born with two holes in her heart at 31 weeks, weighing only 2 pounds. She does in fact have Down syndrome. Finley is a remarkably beautiful human being, and I had nothing to fear. People with Down syndrome are gifts to be celebrated and perfectly created in the image of God. I pray you get to love and be loved by someone with Down syndrome.

The Gift

Between the recent diagnosis of our newest baby, morning sickness (which is never sequestered to the first part of the day), extreme fatigue, the daily bickering among my three children, the obnoxious tantrums, the never-ending complaints, frequent solo parenting, nightly sleep interruptions, regular shouts of "It's not fair!" and accusations of being "the worst mom ever," I'm tempted to laugh in utter disbelief when God tells us that children are a gift from the Lord. However, Psalm 127:3–4 (NIV) clearly states this truth:

> Children are a heritage from the LORD,
> offspring a reward from him.
> Like arrows in the hands of a warrior
> are children born in one's youth.

All children, regardless of gender or health condition, are intentionally and intricately woven by the hand of God (Ps. 139:13). The Hebrew word for "heritage" is *naḥălâ*, which means "gift, inheritance, or heirloom." Verse 3 even reveals that children are a reward! When the enemy attempts to deceive us into believing anything other than this truth, and he will, returning to the Word of God grounds us in fact—the fact that each child the Lord *gifts* you with is a *reward*.

Next, God tells us that our children are similar to arrows in the hands of warriors. *You* are the warrior. The Hebrew word for "warrior" means "valiant, mighty, strong, champion." On those days when you feel defeated and depleted as a parent, recall that God entrusts you as a warrior with an arrow in your hand. As parents, we play a vital role in how our "arrow will fly." Bible scholar David Guzik explains this metaphor:

- They must be carefully shaped and formed.
- They must be guided with skill and strength.
- They must be given care, or they will not fly straight.
- They must be aimed and given direction; they will not find direction on their own.

- They are, in some respects, only launched once.
- They are an extension of the warrior's strength and accomplishment.
- They have potential for much good or evil.[1]

God gave us our children, unique as they are, to bless us. Yet we have a paramount responsibility to steward our gift of children. They are to be shaped and used for the Lord's kingdom purposes.

As we've read, children are a gift from the Lord, but God also uses them to gift us with something else: sanctification. As we've already learned, sanctification is a purification process that ultimately forms us into the image of Christ. Said another way, it's a lifelong journey of becoming more like Jesus. Of course, we'll never get there fully on this side of heaven, but if we partner with God's plans, we'll continually be sanctified in our walk with the Lord, reflecting the character of Christ more and more.

Outside of marriage, I believe God uses parenting as another major way to purify and sanctify us. Paul Tautges, a counselor with the Association of Certified Biblical Counselors, explains the purification process:

> The picture here is of an ancient goldsmith who puts his crude gold ore in a crucible, subjects it to intense heat, and thus liquefies the mass. The impurities rise to the surface and are skimmed off. When the metalworker is able to see the reflection of his face clearly mirrored in the surface of the liquid, he takes it off the fire, for he knows that the contents are pure gold.

The point is clear: God uses suffering to heat
up our lives in order to bring the scum of our
hearts into full view in order that we may repent
and be refined—to reflect more accurately the
beauty of Jesus.[2]

Isaiah 48:10 says, "Look, I have refined you, but not as silver;
I have tested you in the furnace of affliction." Can we all agree
that parenting is sometimes a furnace of affliction? Maybe that
sounds harsh to you if you have gentle, obedient children, but
the Lord gave me spirited and challenging children, and I have
felt the burning temperatures of the furnace. Yet, in His grace,
He continually refines me in the parenting furnace. The personal
growth I've seen in my eleven years of parenting is a testament
to God's expert skill; however, the Lord knows I still have a long
way to go!

Biblical scholar Charles Spurgeon explains that silver refin-
ing is one of the most skilled works of man, but the Lord's divine
wisdom and artistry far exceed this skill of man.[3] Thus, this analogy shows us that the challenges God allows us to encounter for
purification are done with sincere thought and intention.

The Problem

Children are sinners. I know, shocking! As much as it would
be nice to believe babies are born naturally good, they're not.
As descendants of Adam and Eve, they have inherited a sinful
nature, just as you and I inherited. We don't have to teach our
kids to whine, manipulate, hit, kick, disobey, and lie. It comes
naturally. Throw in a military kid's transient and unpredictable

life, and their sins likely dramatically increase as they attempt to process their emotions. This creates *a lot* of problems for us as parents.

But we create *many* problems for our kids because we are also inherently sinful. We struggle with anger, discontent, resentment, impatience, and frustration—to name a few. Magnify my everyday human struggles with the added pressure of deployment, extended field training, and my spouse's excessive work hours, and how can I possibly succeed as a parent? It starts with acceptance and repentance.

I never knew I had a problem with anger until I had children! Anyone else? The unexplainable heat that rose in my body during a kid's tantrum, an act of overt disobedience, or deliberate harm to a sibling transformed me into what felt like an evil ruler for a few moments. I didn't even recognize myself, and the fear in my kids' eyes revealed my error. What is happening?!

I recognized I couldn't parent my children in my own strength. No matter how many books, podcasts, seminars, or online courses I consumed (which was a lot!), I couldn't educate myself into being a perfect parent. Sure, what I learned helped and shifted my parenting choices, but more than anything, I needed constant communion with the Lord and an open heart to the Holy Spirit's leading.

I learned the necessity of apologizing to my children and modeling the need to ask for forgiveness when I mess up. What a life skill to teach our children—owning up to our mistakes and seeking reconciliation. I'm thankful the Lord taught me this lesson early on because my children will grow up hearing regular apologies as I daily miss the mark, and they'll see me try to realign myself with God's will.

The act of apologizing is translating to their lives, not always quickly but in time, as they apologize to the person they've offended and seek to right their wrong. And this is practice for what we need to do daily with Jesus: admit our sins and realign our hearts with His will.

So the parenting problem we're going to come up against again and again and again is sin. The inherited sin we didn't choose—sin in your kids, sin in your husband, and sin within yourself. And, of course, the enemy desires to keep you stuck deep within sin's confines.

The Solution

As I said earlier, you can't educate or will yourself out of the problem of sin. So, unfortunately, we're all stuck with it until we reach heaven. But by the grace of God, there is hope.

When Christ came to earth to pay the penalties for our sins by dying on the cross, He opened the door for grace, a gift God offers us that we do not deserve. As believers in the birth, death, and resurrection of Jesus, God now sees us as pure and sinless. It's as if Christ's death put a filter in front of the Lord's eyes that absolves the sins of His adopted sons and daughters as Jesus constantly intercedes for us (Rom. 8:34).

As part of God's family, we have the blessing of being able to confess our sins and be forgiven daily. Lamentations 3:22–23 (ESV) states: "The steadfast love of the LORD never ceases; his mercies never come to an end; they are new every morning; great is your faithfulness." We get a perpetual do-over every twenty-four hours.

The grace of God is our solution to sin. The blood Jesus shed so we could enjoy the blessings of forgiveness and eternal life is the solution to our sin. The Savior is the solution to your child's sin. The Messiah is the solution to your husband's sin. The King of kings is the solution to your sin. His grace is there for the taking every time you need it, and even when you fall, He never tires of helping you get back up and take your next step toward healing, wholeness, and righteousness.

Your Job as a Parent

Modern society has created a unique pressure that leads us to believe our kids must excel at everything—fine arts, sports, academics, social interactions, emotional intelligence, and so on. While those things can be beneficial, my job is not to ensure they succeed in all those arenas. Instead, I think my role as a parent is to teach my kids one foundational lesson, and everything else hinges on their acceptance of this one lesson: God is trustworthy.

So, how do we teach our kids that God is trustworthy?

Modeling

God chose *you* to parent *your* children for a reason. Your experiences, personality traits, weaknesses, and gifts all matter to your child's development. He has entrusted *you* to model what a healthy relationship with Jesus looks like.

If you don't have a personal relationship with Jesus, start seeking Him. Read the Bible, read other Christian books, listen to Christian music and podcasts, pray, attend church, and ask the

Lord to reveal Himself to you, and He will be faithful to show You who He is in His timing (Matt. 7:7–8).

If you know Jesus and accept Him as your Savior, the Lord desires you to be on fire for His kingdom. He wants you to follow Him diligently. None of this lukewarm stuff (Rev. 3:15–16). He wants you all in as a follower of Christ.

The following actions can help you model a thriving relationship with Christ:

- Reading or listening to the Bible daily
- Studying the Word of God
- Praying
- Attending and serving in your local church
- Intentionally loving those around you and in your community
- Investing in your marriage
- Seeking God's will
- Obeying God's will
- Being an active part of a small group or Bible study

This list is not all-inclusive, but it's an excellent place to start and evaluate your walk with God. You've heard it said before: "Our kids do what we do, not what we say." But remember to give yourself grace when life happens. You're not going to mess up your kid by not modeling a "perfect" relationship with Jesus when you're in the middle of packing up your house, your spouse just deployed, and you're still adjusting to solo parenting, or you stayed up too late to enjoy some time to yourself and didn't get to your morning Bible reading.

If you are modeling a life that follows Jesus, you'll naturally lead into living a Deuteronomy 6:6–7 (NIV) lifestyle. This verse gives us a beautiful and full picture of our biblical parenting goals: "These commandments that I give you today are to be on your hearts. Impress them on your children. Talk about them when you sit at home and when you walk along the road, when you lie down and when you get up."

We need to know the Word, teach it to our kids, and discuss it. *All. The. Time.* That might feel intimidating, but it's relatively easy to recognize God's hand and handiwork once you walk with Him closely. After that, you'll start seeing Him everywhere.

You can start your morning by reading God's Word together and listening to worship music. Talk about God's instructions and how Jesus acted as you work through your child's behavior issues. Pray before meals. Attribute a flower's beauty or a sunset's magnificence to God's artistry. Marvel at His creativity and provision as you watch the variety of birds on your bird feeder. Pray together before bedtime, praising God, thanking Him, repenting from your sins, praying for others, and asking for God's help.

Teach Your Kids Their God-given Mission

Knowing that we have a purposeful mission helps us trust God when we don't understand our circumstances. There's a reason He moved your kids to Alaska or Germany, or Korea, or Louisiana. There are people the Lord needs your kids to love and serve there!

No matter a believer's age, we all have the same mission: love God and love others. Point your kids to Matthew 22:37–39, where Jesus defines the most important commandments in the law: "Love the Lord your God with all your heart, with all your soul, and with all your mind. This is the greatest and most important command. The second is like it: Love your neighbor as yourself."

When my kids are being selfish, I often ask a simple question that turns things around: "Are you being loving right now?" It enables them to do a quick heart check without my condemnation. A follow-up question I tend to ask is, "What do you think Jesus would do in that situation?" Because my kids are exposed to the Scriptures daily, they know Christ's character and can see when their behavior doesn't align with His.

As followers of Christ, God also calls our kids to fulfill the Great Commission, a command given by Jesus to His disciples in Matthew 28:19–20: "Go, therefore, and make disciples of all nations, baptizing them in the name of the Father and of the Son and of the Holy Spirit, teaching them to observe everything I have commanded you." Do not underestimate the power of your children to fulfill this command. I often hear our kids talking about God on the playground, sports field, and on playdates with military and civilian kids. They're starting beautiful conversations and planting seeds the Lord will nurture.

Finally, get them involved in serving the military community where God's placed them. Here are a few suggestions:

- Babysit the children of a friend with a deployed spouse.
- Mow the lawn or shovel snow for a neighbor with a deployed spouse.
- Invite new neighbors over for a playdate.
- Have your kids help you cook a meal for a neighbor who is sick.

- Write thank-you cards to deployed service members.
- Send a Christmas package to a deployed unit.
- Lay wreaths or place flags at a veterans' cemetery.

Unified Parenting

No question, parenting is the number one source of conflict in my marriage! Can you relate? Due to different disciplinary styles growing up, our unique personalities, our varied levels of parental education (my husband doesn't have time to sit around and read all the latest parenting books!), and my husband's on-and-off presence at home due to his work schedule, we have regular disagreements about parenting.

To get on the same parenting page (or at least in the same book!), Tim and I have taken an online parenting course, read a few books, listened to a parenting podcast, and worked with a family counselor. All of which I highly recommend. These steps helped us to come to an agreement on our mutual parenting style.

We don't have it all figured out, and I'm convinced we never will, but we at least understand we're on the same team and have the same objectives. Most importantly, we've learned to apologize (to each other and the kids) when we overstep or mess up.

If your spouse is not a believer, your parenting journey may be significantly more difficult because you have different foundations. Yet God knows your spouse's heart and still chose to join you together. So, as his wife, respect your husband's views on parenting, ask his opinions, and try his suggestions (as long as they don't go against the Lord). Your consideration of him shows the light of Jesus (see 1 Cor. 7:12–16).

Transition

Many of our kids live in a perpetual state of transition. After our last move to Fort Liberty, my kids had officially lived in as many houses as they were old. My then eight-year-old had lived in eight homes. My six-year-old had lived in six homes. My four-year-old had lived in four homes. That's ridiculous.

As I mentioned in a previous chapter, one of my children, who struggled with behavioral and emotional challenges, was diagnosed with transition disorder. I didn't even know that was a thing! I couldn't help but feel like we were damaging our child.

As I type these words, we're approaching the sixteen-year mark in the military. Even though we've been able to "stabilize" for three years here at Fort Liberty, my children are still experiencing a constant transition. Nearly every month or two, my husband leaves for a field exercise, advanced training, or a planning mission. Sometimes he's gone for two days, sometimes a week, and other times a month. He's also gone one night each week to maintain his night flying qualifications as an Apache pilot. At least a few nights per week, he misses dinner with us, but thankfully we typically have our weekends together unless he's away training.

All this change and living in a state of never knowing what to expect causes emotional challenges for my kids and me. We live in repeated cycles of disappointment, surprise, and excitement. *You're coming home for dinner?! That's amazing. You're going to miss Adeline's performance? Not again.* Somewhere along the way, I heard a parenting expert say that handling disappointment is the most important thing we can teach our children. If that's true, God is allowing our children a plethora of opportunities to mature in this area!

My stability in all this change and transition is the One who never changes, God. So, when we sit around the dinner table, frustrated that Tim's chair is empty, we talk about the vital work God needs Daddy to do. We talk about how He calls us to serve as a military family, which requires sacrifice. We talk about how God is good and His plans are for our good (Rom. 8:28). When your children (and you) battle the effects of transition, I pray you each find peace in trusting the One who has called you to this lifestyle.

A Father's Absence

Solo parenting is part of the contract for being a military wife. No, there's not an actual contract, but if there was, you can bet an agreement to solo parenting would be in section II, clause A. Regarding parenting, here are some ideas to help your children adjust.

- Prepare them ahead of time for their dad's absence, if you have advance notice.
- Order a cardboard cutout of your service member to help keep his presence around. (I did this for our oldest daughter, who was two months old when Tim deployed. Note: never leave the cutout sitting in a chair at

the kitchen table. It'll freak you out when you come around the corner!)

- Look for deployment resources on your local installation. Many have options like classes for kids, a place for your husband to record a video reading a book to your child, and blankets or stuffed animals to comfort your child.

- Try to video chat with your service member as often as possible.

- Order a daddy doll for younger kids (a plush doll with a place to insert your husband's photo or a stuffed doll with his image printed on it).

- Go to Build-A-Bear before the deployment and allow your child to create a stuffed animal. Have your husband record a message on an audio button insert so your child can press it and hear Dad's voice when he's away.

- If possible, discuss parenting decisions with your husband while he is away.

Reintegration

I don't know about you, but I had no idea that reintegration (the period after a service member returns home) would be anything other than sheer glee. Often, it's more on the messy side and less celebratory than the public envisions. Everyone has to learn to live with another person's opinion, schedule, and quirks again. Also, kids must adjust to their dad also being in charge when he returns; it's no longer all Mom's way. The rules and expectations may be different, and that change is hard!

Prepare your kids before your husband returns by discussing how it might be challenging when their dad gets home. For example, he will likely need to sleep a lot, naps included, and may not be able to play as much as they anticipate. In addition, he might have low energy and need time alone to recover.

But also, plan some fun activities ahead of time that everyone can look forward to doing. This allows your family to create new memories! One of our favorite ways to do this is by giving our kids a "Yes Day." Like the movie by the same name, allow your kids to plan the day (with boundaries given in advance), and you and your husband "have" to say yes to anything they suggest. Our kids *love* this!

Common Struggles

Your kids will likely not be immune to the stressors of military life. You may see flickers of negative emotions and behaviors, or like me, you may feel like you've barely got your neck above the torrent rivers of childhood trauma. Most days, I'm grasping for any floating driftwood to keep me from heading over the waterfall.

Anxiety, anger, fear, sadness, depression, and loneliness are typical struggles our military children battle. But, of course, our children's generation faces these problems at large, civilian or military. Still, as with everything in military life, the armed forces' stressors exacerbate life's everyday challenges.

What can we do to help our military children not only *survive* but *thrive* amid these struggles?

Here are a few suggestions:

- Teach them to turn to God with their big emotions. Lead them to prayer and Scripture.
- Teach them to meditate on God's character.
- Teach them that this mission field comes with tribulation and that God wants to use them here to love and help others and will equip them to do so.
- Enroll your child in counseling, preferably with a Christian counselor.
- Look into bringing an emotional therapy dog into your home.
- Help your children cultivate friendships to support them.
- Get involved in community groups on post that support military kids with fun camps, classes, and activities.

Taking Care of Yourself

The term *self-care* has some negative connotations, and I understand why, but there's a difference between interpreting that term as an excuse to do whatever you want whenever you want and interpreting it as a reminder to regularly stop and embrace the fact that *you're not God*. As a mother with challenging kids, I *need time* to recharge and recuperate, reminding myself that I'm a limited creature and not the Creator. There is nothing wrong with that. Thankfully, my husband understands my need for rest and takes care of our children on most Saturdays so that I can catch my breath. During my time alone on Saturdays, I might walk, meet with friends, run errands, pray, soak in the bath, nap, read a book, watch a movie, or paint my nails.

In her book, *Scoot Over and Make Some Room*, Heather Avis explains the idea of rest this way:

> Rest is not about doing what we want when we want to because we deserve it, but about recognizing our need for a God-ordained pause. A pause that requires us to step away from our hands-on job as a mom long enough to reconnect with the heart of God—which in turn helps us be a better mom, wife, friend, and human being.[4]

Additionally, part of taking care of yourself is having a support system you can call on when you need companionship, advice, help with an emergency, or when it's time for you to rest and your husband is away on duty! Start cultivating this group as soon as you get to a new location. You're going to need them!

Your support system may consist of neighbors, parents, friends, spouses clubs, women in your husband's unit, people at your church, a book club, your kid's coaches or teachers, counselors, and doctors. You know that "it takes a village" to do military life well. God didn't design us to do this on our own, sister!

Relying on God's Character

Our military children may not know worldly stability as much as we desire to give it to them. Still, they can understand the everlasting stability of the Lord, a far greater experience.

When the Lord tells them to pack up and leave their friends, the Lord remains their greatest friend.

> "I do not call you servants anymore, because a servant doesn't know what his master is doing. I have called you friends, because I have made known to you everything I have heard from my Father." (John 15:15)

When they hug their daddy before he loads a bus headed to a war-torn country, the Lord remains faithful.

> Your steadfast love, O LORD, extends to
> the heavens,
> your faithfulness to the clouds.
> (Ps. 36:5 ESV)

When they sit in a doctor's office receiving a diagnosis of anxiety, depression, or transition disorder, the Lord remains their comforter and healer.

> Praise be to the God and Father of our Lord Jesus Christ, the Father of compassion and the God of all comfort, who comforts us in all our troubles, so that we can comfort those in any trouble with the comfort we ourselves receive from God. (2 Cor. 1:3–4 NIV)

The ever-shifting boundaries of military life find their stability in the one true God who never changes: "Jesus Christ never changes! He is the same yesterday, today, and forever" (Heb. 13:8 CEV). Although Jesus remains the same, God doesn't want our kids (or us) to stay the same. Instead, He desires for us to shift, change, transition, and grow. If we partner with Him, He can use our challenges in the military to transform us into the image of Christ.

Before we look at modeling Jesus, I want to share a true story about the "winds of life" with you. On a *Celebrate Kids* podcast episode, host Kathy Koch gave an illustration that teaches us that "wind" is necessary and beneficial in our kids' lives. Near my hometown of Tucson, Arizona, sits Biosphere 2, "the world's largest controlled environment dedicated to understanding the impacts of climate change." This man-made indoor research facility houses a variety of simulated natural environments: the ocean, the rainforest, the desert, the tropics, and the savannah.

Researchers couldn't figure out why the trees indoors at Biosphere 2 kept falling. They'd reach a certain height and then fall over and die. What was wrong? In real nature, trees are exposed to storms. It turns out that trees *need* turbulent winds to strengthen themselves. The wind *helps* their roots grow deeper and *aids* in their protective bark growing thicker! This military life can have the same maturing effect on our kids.

Do you want to embrace this perspective with me? I find great hope in knowing that God doesn't thoughtlessly throw parenting storms at us to knock us over; He wants to deepen our "roots" in Him and strengthen our protective shields of faith. He doesn't want us to fall over in the long run, so He sends wind every now and then to help us develop strength. What a good Father.

Modeling Jesus: Children Are a Welcome Gift

Finally, we turn to Jesus's view on children with the goal of parenting so that our children feel like they are gifts from our heavenly Father as we intentionally lead them to the Savior. While Jesus was in Judea, surrounded by huge crowds and healing them, the Pharisees (religious leaders) began asking him questions to test Him. Following His response to their questions, people began to bring children to Jesus so He could lay hands on them and pray.

Can't you imagine yourself doing the same—after all our children endure as military children, I'd be pushing them forward to encounter the blessings and healing of Jesus! Jesus's disciples, however, didn't think the children were worthy of Jesus's precious time and energy, so they rebuked them. But Jesus, in His wisdom and kindness, said: "'Leave the little children alone, and don't try to keep them from coming to me, because the kingdom of heaven belongs to such as these.' After placing his hands on them, he went on from there" (Matt. 19:14–15).

Those children must have felt very significant at that moment and forever afterward! I pray that despite all our exhaustion from moving, transitions, setting up new homes and new communities, serving others, working, and solo parenting, we are never too weary to bring our children to the feet of Jesus. Our Savior tells us this is of paramount importance.

Prayer

Dear Heavenly Father,

You have created each of us in Your image, wonderfully and remarkably. You are the ultimate parent, loving me and disciplining me far better than I could ever attempt to do for my children. Thank You for gifting me with the Scriptures and the Holy Spirit to guide me as I parent the children You have entrusted to me. Please help me raise them in a way that honors and glorifies Your name. I also ask for Your help in disciplining my children, Lord. Show me when to offer mercy, where to set boundaries, and how to provide consequences that matter. Give me a contagious passion for You and Your Word that draws my children to You. Please help me identify the gifts You've given them so I can steward them for Your kingdom purposes. Lord, I want to avoid getting lost in what the culture says is important about raising kids. May I consciously turn to what You say about parenting instead. God, I know You have placed my children within the boundaries of the armed services for a reason. Come alongside me in showing this truth to my kids. We love You, Father. In Jesus's guiding name, amen.

Reflection Questions

1. What is the most challenging part of parenting for you?

2. Did you have a positive role model for parenting growing up? If not, is there someone around you whose parenting you admire and whom you can ask to mentor you?

3. What areas of parenting are a source of contention for you and your husband?

4. In what areas do you excel as a parent? In what areas do you want to mature as a parent?

5. Write down your children's names and the gifts you recognize God's given them. How can you help them steward those unique gifts for God's glory?

6. Have you surrendered your parenting and your children to the Lord? If not, write a prayer handing them over to God.

—————————— *Next Steps* ——————————

❑ Ask God to reveal areas of your parenting where He wants you to grow.
❑ Give yourself grace when you make mistakes in your parenting.
❑ Embrace new mercies each morning.
❑ Purchase or borrow military-related literature for your children (suggestions below).

—————————— *Resources* ——————————

For links and descriptions of each resource, visit Ashleyashcraft.com/missionreadymarriage.

- *Parenting* by Paul David Tripp
- *8 Great Smarts* by Kathy Koch
- *The Explosive Child* by Ross W. Greene, PhD
- *Gist* by Timothy D. Johanson, MD and Michael W. Anderson, LP

- *Risen Motherhood* by Emily Jensen and Laura Wifler
- *Mama Bear Apologetics* by Hillary Ferrer
- *Raising Emotionally Strong Boys* by David Thomas, LMSW
- *Raising Worry-Free Girls* by Sissy Goff, MEd, LPC-MHSP
- *The 5 Love Languages of Children* by Gary Chapman and Ross Campbell
- *Keeping Your Kids on God's Side* by Natasha Crain
- *The Explorer Bible*
- *Jesus Storybook Bible* by Sally Lloyd Jones
- *Calm Parenting* podcast
- *Truth Seekers* podcast
- *Moms in Prayer* podcast
- *Parenting Great Kids* podcast
- *Raising Girls and Boys* podcast
- *Connected Families* podcast
- *Mom to Mom* podcast
- *Military Child Education Coalition* podcast
- Lectio for Families app
- Armed Services Ministry Hero Squad
- Club Beyond
- Counting Our Heroes Home Subscription Box
- The Comfort Crew for Military Kids
- Military Child Education Coalition
- Student 2 Student
- Sesame Street for Military Families

Picture Books for Military Kids

- *The Lord's Army* by Sheri Rose Shepherd
- *Don't Forget, God Bless Our Troops* by Jill Biden
- *My Daddy Is a Hero* by Hannah Tolson
- *H is for Honor, a Military Family Alphabet* by Devin Scillian
- *Veterans: Heroes in Our Neighborhood* by Valerie Pfundstein
- *Sergeant Billy* by Mireille Messier
- *Otto's Tales: Today is Veterans Day!* by PragerU
- *Sergeant Reckless* by Patricia McCormick
- *Stubby: A True Story of Friendship* by Michael Foreman
- *Stubby: Inspired by the True Story of an American Hero in World War I* by Kathy Borrus
- *Maggie the Military Rat* by Monica Voicu Denniston
- *Papa's Backpack* by James Christopher Carroll
- *The Big Move* by Johanna and Daniel Gomez
- *Myra Prat the Military Brat* by Statasha F. McPhatter
- *My Flight Suit Pocket* by Kathryn Hamlin-Pacheco, OTR/L

Chapter Eleven

Marital Intimacy: Together and Apart

Our biggest challenge with marital
intimacy is _____.

Have you ever felt the urgent need to revive yourself from your own dissatisfaction? After settling in from our eleventh move while raising three kids under the age of seven and recovering from the emotional upheaval of a miscarriage, I couldn't sit in my discontent any longer.

I didn't want to blame Tim for the hardships of this lifestyle for another second. I was ready to take responsibility for my attitudes and actions and start intentionally loving like Jesus, unconditionally. With fresh hope, I created a forty-day challenge to extravagantly love and selflessly serve Tim. I needed to take the focus off myself and freely pour into my husband. Coming up with fun and meaningful ways to love him evoked a sweet joy I had been missing.

Over the next forty days, we experienced a level of intimacy we had not previously known. And when the last challenge commenced, Tim vowed to create his own forty-day challenge for me so our newfound connection could continue. Instead of staying stuck in my negativity toward my husband and his profession (which I did for a decade, despite loving him immensely), I made a commitment to invest in my marital intimacy. Modeling Jesus transformed my heart, and the results were undeniable.

What Is Intimacy?

God designed people to be in close communion, or relationship, with each other and Him. However, considering the modern culture that aims to connect us with as many people as possible through social media, I must note that God did not design us for intimate relationships with hundreds of people, let alone thousands. You cannot have deep, authentic relationships that mirror the love of God with that many people—it's impossible. This is because to have an intimate relationship with someone, you need to *know* them. In the Bible, the Hebrew word for "know" is *yada*.

Pastor Sam Yoon explains further:

> The Hebrew word yada is a verb that means to know, to be known and to be deeply respected. It can represent sex but also goes beyond that to signify an incredibly deep sense of intimacy, vulnerability, and connection between two people. In fact, this word is used over 900 times in the Old Testament, including instances that

describe how God "yada" (knows and respects)
us deeply.[1]

In your covenant relationship with your husband, God has
given you the gift of "yada" so that others can "yada" Him.
Marriage is supposed to be a visible picture for ourselves and
others of Christ's divine love for his church. The union between
ourselves and our spouses is both a gift and a symbol to point
us toward Him, toward His love (Eph. 5:32). While all aspects
of the marriage union are part of this spiritual symbol, sexual
intimacy is a part we usually forget to consider a spiritual act.
And yet it is! When we experience all that a marital union entails,
including intimacy, we are telling the story of the "oneness" Jesus
has with His bride, the church. As we discuss marital intimacy in
this chapter, I'll be referring to a gift of closeness and complete
knowing that only a husband and wife share, representing the
genuine love of God. Intimacy is a by-product of connection,
and as husband and wife, we can do that in various ways, like
communication, vulnerability, and sexuality.

Why Does Marital Intimacy Matter?

In their book *Male and Female: Embracing Your Role in
God's Design*, authors Jonathan Petzold and Christa Petzold state
that "Christians live out faithful, loving, forgiving marriages for
Gospel proclamation."[2] Your marital intimacy matters because
it has the opportunity to proclaim the gospel! That is not something to take lightly.

As believers in Christ, God commands us to share the truth
of Jesus with others. Where we share the gospel will look different

for each of us based on our life circumstances. You may be sharing the gospel with a mom at football practice, your neighbors, a customer at your job, the parents in your special needs support group, or a community on social media. But, as wives, we share this in common: God calls us to proclaim the gospel by the way we love our husbands.

Are You Really Experiencing Marital Intimacy?

A couple of years ago, I realized I didn't view my husband as my best friend anymore—a painful reality. As someone naturally independent, I managed our family "successfully" during my husband's frequent absences due to work. I developed my own routines to care for the house and the kids. Without his input or his ever-changing schedule to work around, I had us operating predictably and effectively.

Practically, I was doing fine. But relationally, I was hurting and distant. Between Tim's excessive work hours and regular absences, I learned to share my thoughts and feelings with God and friends, both great things but not when it meant I stopped confiding in my husband.

I also noticed I was holding in my emotions when Tim was around. If something bothered me, I'd cry in the bathroom, wait until I could compose myself, and then come out without him ever knowing something was wrong.

That's when I realized something needed to change. I confessed this to my husband and began to share my feelings and dreams with him again. I had to figure out how to allow him into my world, even though he frequently left it due to his job.

My vulnerability was necessary to establish our marital intimacy again.

When your marital intimacy is lacking, you may falsely satisfy your need for intimacy from another source. Here are a few ways you or your spouse may be experiencing false marital intimacy:

- Pornography
- Lust with your partner, not love
- Romantic literature or movies
- Getting all of your emotional needs met through friends, family members, or your kids (It's not wrong to connect with your friends and family emotionally, of course! The question is this: Are you getting a disproportionate amount of your emotional needs met in them, crowding out any chance to experience this with your husband?)

Spend some time in prayer asking God if there are any areas in your marriage where you are experiencing false marital intimacy.

Intimacy through Communication

While at Fort Leavenworth, Tim was approached to fulfill a job within a special operations sect of the Army. If he accepted the position, he'd be gone on numerous unknown missions, and I wouldn't know where he was in the world or for how long he would be gone. That was too wild for me to entertain!

But for some of you reading this book, that is your reality. Your husband is gone regularly, and you don't know where he is, when he'll be back, or when you'll get to speak to him next. Yet, even if your husband isn't in special forces, he's still likely gone several times yearly for training. And even if he's not away on duty geographically, it often feels that way because he gets home so late and often returns to work mode once he's home.

How do we foster communication in our marriages considering all these factors? As research for this book, I've read dozens of marriage books. Whenever I get to a communication section, I laugh at the impossibility of the suggestions. Wise advice sits on those pages but doesn't apply to military couples. We can't have dinner together every night or even most nights. We often can't spend thirty minutes together each day talking. We don't have the opportunity to share our feelings openly on any given day. And on I could go. It's different for us.

Yet we must find a way to work around the constraints of our time together as military couples. We have to fight for it. And it will look different for each of us, depending on your husband's current position, rank, responsibilities, location, and so on.

The military trains our husbands to multitask in their profession, and as women, most of us are highly proficient in the sport, but that doesn't work with marital communication. A critical key to your time together as a couple is that it needs to be distraction free: no cell phones, televisions, computers, kids, books, magazines, and so forth. Try to schedule a time to talk to each other each day, considering your current state of life.

If he's deployed, you know that means always keeping your phone by you because you never know when he'll have a free moment to talk. If he's TDY (temporary duty), he may call each night at the same time. If he's currently stationed at home but in a demanding position, you might schedule ten minutes each night after the kids are asleep before he has to start working again.

We'll all inevitably go through periods when we cannot talk with our husbands. They may be serving in a secretive location abroad, have no cell signal in the field, or enduring their three weeks at survival school where communication isn't permitted. To bridge the communication gap, consider documenting your days and thoughts in a letter or email to share with your husband when he returns.

Intimacy through Quality Time

We may only get bits of time to communicate here and there, but when we can, we need to build in quality time to invest in our marital intimacy. When your husband is home, consider coming up with a routine date night; once a week is ideal. However, in my husband's current position, we only go out once a month.

One of the huge challenges in dating as a military couple is that we don't usually have family around us that can babysit for free, and paying a babysitter gets expensive! So consider swapping babysitting with another couple to ensure a regular date night. Also, think of dates that go beyond the typical dinner and a movie occasionally. New experiences together build bonding connections in our brains.

Finally, try to plan one kid-free vacation each year. I know there may be a hundred factors that make that feel impossible, but figuring out how to make it happen is imperative for marital intimacy. Even if you can only do it every other year, fight for it.

It checks the box for new experiences, sexual intimacy, quality time, and no kids!

With my husband's current job, we could only get away for one night this year. I was disappointed, but you understand better than anyone. However, at other duty stations, we've had more luck. After Tim's first deployment, we vacationed for two weeks (before the kids and when we had two incomes). Your couple's vacation will look different in each season, but try to prioritize it! It'll be worth it.

Intimacy through Education

I'm an enthusiastic learner by nature. I want to know how to improve everything I do and everything I'm a part of, my marriage included. So, over the last year, I've been piling books on my husband's side of the bed that I can't wait for him to read about marriage and parenting. Do you know how many he's read? None. And I can't blame him. He literally has no time to read.

Last week, while I cleaned our bedroom, I removed all the books I wanted him to read and placed them on our bookshelf in the living room. It's not the right time for him to read as a way of learning. As a brigade operations officer, he basically has time to work and . . . work. Maybe he'll have some free time in his next position, so while we wait for that, I will share what I read with him verbally. He's also discovered that podcasts are an excellent way to learn right now. On his twenty-minute drive to work, or as he drives to different meetings around the post, he often listens to a podcast on faith, marriage, or parenting.

We will never learn everything we need to know about our partners or marriage on this side of heaven. Still, it's crucial to better ourselves and our marriage as much as possible because it's how we proclaim the gospel! I once heard a podcast interviewee discuss the importance of investing in our marriage through education. He suggested that each year we read one book together, attend one conference that will advance our marriage, listen to the same podcast and discuss it, and take a couple's vacation.

The word *education* may feel dull when you think about intimacy, but you can get creative if you or your husband need enticing. Here are a few ideas to make it enjoyable:

- Read a book aloud while you sit in the bath together.
- Massage him while he reads a chapter out loud.
- Take turns reading while naked in bed.
- Stay in a hotel together during the conference, even if it's just for one night.
- Try out the suggestions you each learned about from the podcast episode.

Intimacy through Sexuality

Unfortunately, I did not understand God's beautiful design for sexual intimacy when Tim and I pledged our vows. Outside of the Bible, one of the most impactful resources my husband and I have used to help us figure this out is Dr. Juli Slattery's podcast Java with Juli, a ministry of Authentic Intimacy.

Authentic Intimacy's mission is to "reclaim God's design for sexuality." During our time at West Point and Fort Leavenworth, Tim and I regularly listened to Dr. Slattery's podcast. Through her biblical wisdom and the many experts she interviewed, we finally began to understand (and practice!) God's design for sexuality. I'd mark our time learning from Authentic Intimacy as a drastic turning point in our marriage. Secrets were shared, hurts began to heal, counselors were called in to help us process our past, and sex gradually became the gift God intended.

Sex first appears on the scene in Genesis 4:1: "The man was intimate with his wife Eve, and she conceived and gave birth to Cain. She said, 'I have had a male child with the LORD's help.'" The original Hebrew word used for intimate is *yada*. Remember that word from earlier? It means "to know and be known." We learned that it also signifies an incredibly deep sense of intimacy, vulnerability, and connection between two people.

Sam Yoon explains that "Yada shows us that God's gift of sex is more than just a purely physical and pleasurable act—it is part of a deeper gift of intimacy God desires for us to have in marriage. Godly sex, yada, is not just being physically naked but also being emotionally and spiritually naked with your spouse."[3]

I wish you could see my copy of Christopher West's book *Our Bodies Tell God's Story*. Just about every other page is dog-eared, and almost every page is thoroughly highlighted. This book should be required reading for every human being as it boldly details God's design for sex within marriage. How different could our world look if we all knew why God created sex?

Paul calls sexuality a "profound mystery" (Eph. 5:32 NIV), yet God is not a God of confusion. Within the pages of the Bible, He's laid out His guidance on sex to protect us, ensure we honor Him with our bodies, and enjoy the mutual blessings of marital sexuality. But unfortunately, most people don't take the time to seek His will and obey His commands. And when we do sex apart from God, there are often catastrophic consequences.

Thankfully, Christopher West offers us great insight into our sexuality when he writes:

> Behind every false god we discover our desire for the true God gone awry. The sexual confusion so prevalent in our world and in our own hearts is actually the human desire for heaven gone berserk. Untwist the distortions and we discover the astounding glory of sex in the divine plan. "For this reason . . . the two shall become one flesh" (Matt. 19:5; cf. Gen. 2:34). For what reason? To reveal, proclaim, and anticipate the eternal union of Christ and the church.[4]

When a man and woman become one sexually, they are creating an image, a symbol, an analogy. Their physical communion (which is meant to be a willing gift to each other) is supposed to represent the love Jesus (sometimes referred to as the "heavenly Bridegroom" in the Bible) has for us. Are you giving yourself willingly in love to your husband as a gift? Is your husband willingly giving himself to you as a gift, and is it one you want to receive because you trust him?

What's NOT God's Design for Sexual Intimacy

Unfortunately, some denominations of Christianity have completely skewed God's plan for sexuality, teaching men to dominate their wives unlovingly. In these sects, wives are called to complete submission regardless of the selfish and lustful intentions of their husbands. This is not God's plan in marriage.

In Ephesians 5:25, husbands are called to "love your wives, just as Christ loved the church and gave himself for her." Verse 29 explains that husbands need to care and provide for their wives as Christ did for the church. Men are to selflessly and sacrificially love their wives as Jesus loves us. He is not to demand, demean, and lust after his wife. One of my dear friends grew up in the Christian culture I mentioned above and was taught that men would stray unless you were a "sanctified" prostitute. I can't imagine how deeply this breaks the Lord's heart and yet brings a sickening smile to the face of our enemy.

You see, when sin entered the world, lust walked right in beside it. The symbol of sex fell from pointing to God to pointing to oneself. Christopher West says,

> As fallen human beings we will be able to sense the pull of lust in our hearts. . . . It's what we do when we experience the pull of lust that matters. Do we seek God's help in resisting it, or do we indulge it? When we indulge it—that is we actively choose "in our hearts" to treat another person as merely an object for our own gratification—we seriously violate that person's dignity and our own. . . . The opposite of love is to use someone as a means to our own selfish end.[5]

The next area of sex I want to address is the lack of sexual passion. God did not design sex as a lifeless interaction between husband and wife. Remember, it's intended as a sign to point to the most profound love that exists! Unfortunately, due to sexual abuse, miseducation, physical pain with sex, hormone imbalance, exhaustion from life stressors, or a host of other issues, you or your husband may be lacking sexual passion.

Yet God does not want you to remain there. I urge you to fight for your marriage in this way. That may include seeing a licensed sex therapist, visiting medical specialists, educating each other on what feels good to ensure arousal, or enrolling in a marriage-intensive counseling weekend. Deep healing often needs to occur before you experience a revival in the bedroom.

But be careful not to think that sexual revival means you need to enact a Hollywood sex scene and if you don't have what the world defines as over-the-top, praiseworthy sex, then your time together is a failure. Passionate sex means you are engaged and receptive to each other. This dynamic looks different for each couple depending on a myriad of factors, and figuring out what works for both of you takes time. So be patient with yourself and your husband. I pray he is open to joining you on this journey.

What Does Intimacy Look like When He's Away?

Before I offer any advice on this topic, let's revisit our definition of *intimacy*: a gift of closeness and complete knowing only shared between a husband and wife that represents the genuine love Christ has for His church. So, when your husband is away on duty, how do you maintain closeness and know each other completely in genuine love?

It's essential that, as a couple, we start with preparation. Typically, we have some notice when our husbands are going to be away, so we can discuss this in advance. Ask him, "How will we maintain intimacy while you're away?" If you are in an assignment where your husband could deploy on short notice, make time to get a plan in place for if/when he deploys.

During this time together, express your desire to sustain your intimacy while he is away and share your ideas. If you like written communication, keep a journal, send letters, or compose emails. Once he's "in country," he may be able to provide you with a time that he can regularly call so you can talk. In addition, video chat helps maintain your connection more since you can see each other.

The "complete knowing" part of this can be difficult with deployments. Your husband likely cannot share all the details of his day while he is gone, but he can record his days in a journal to share them with you later so you know what he's been through. You also may not want to share every frustration of your day, thinking he doesn't need to take on additional stress he cannot help with when he's away. I differ on this, though. I think we need to share what's happening at home so our husbands can comfort us, offer advice, have compassion, and stay informed. Stay in prayer with God, asking for His advice on this. The Holy Spirit will guide you on when and how much to share on any given day.

Next, both husband and wife must have firm boundaries with the opposite sex when the service member is away. (This should also be true when the husband isn't deployed!) Unfortunately, we all probably know someone who has had an affair during deployment, whether that was the service member or the spouse. Protect yourselves against this scheme of the enemy to destroy your family. Decide together what boundaries you'll adhere to. Here are a few examples:

- Don't spend time alone with the opposite sex.
- Don't engage in deep emotional conversation with the opposite sex (this could lead to emotional attachment). Limit your conversation to pleasantries.
- Don't confide in the opposite sex.
- If you are connected on social media with people you were in a former relationship with, unfriend or unfollow them.
- Do not message people of the opposite sex for conversational purposes.

Of course, we have to talk about pornography here because it's a huge pitfall in our society, especially in our military community. In an article titled "The Military Porn Problem," we discover that due to the stressors of military life and frequent separations from family, research shows that our service members are addicted to porn at double the rate of civilians.[6] As you may know, women are also addicted to pornography; this is not solely a male issue!

To properly discuss this topic, I'd need a whole book, so you'll have to turn to other resources I recommend at the end of this chapter for more information, but pornography does not align with the heart of God. It is a dark and twisted version of what God created to symbolize His love. Pornography degrades people, destroys relationships, and advocates for lust, just to name a few deplorable outcomes of engaging in porn. Yet, when our service members deploy, people on the front lines report that almost everyone uses porn. It is a cultural norm.

Pornography is false intimacy, a concept we addressed earlier. In reality, it is the opposite of intimacy. It creates distance between the user and God and the user and their spouse. So I firmly believe this is a topic we must discuss with our husbands before they deploy.

When we're geographically separated and have sexual desires (both husband and wife included), how can we handle those in a manner that glorifies God's intentions for sex? Seek the heart of God and research His intentions on sex further in order to answer that question together.

Getting Help

Let's be honest. Many of us need assistance in the area of intimacy, especially sexual intimacy. Sometimes simply reading a book on the topic can help, but often we require intervention from experienced professionals. If you or your spouse is struggling with intimacy issues, I highly encourage you to seek advice from biblically and clinically informed counselors or programs. And if the first one you work with isn't the right fit, don't give up! Finding the right counselor or program is worth the effort. Your marriage is worth the effort.

Modeling Jesus: Intimacy with the Father

As I've walked with Christ over the last sixteen years, I've discovered an undeniable truth. The closer I walk with God, the more intimacy I cultivate in my marriage. The more I commit to a relationship with the Lord, the more I commit to a relationship with my husband. The two go hand in hand because He has designed our marriages to reflect His love. If we're not seeking God and following His guidance, how will we know how to represent His love in our marriages?

In Matthew 26:36–39, we see a beautiful (and heart-wrenching) scene in a garden after the Last Supper, where Jesus earlier revealed to His twelve disciples His impending death.

> Then Jesus came with them to a place called Gethsemane, and he told the disciples, "Sit here while I go over there and pray." Taking along Peter and the two sons of Zebedee, he began to be sorrowful and troubled. He said to them, "I am deeply grieved to the point of death. Remain here and stay awake with me." Going a little farther, he fell facedown and prayed, "My Father, if it is possible, let this cup pass from me. Yet not as I will, but as you will."

You may recall that we looked at the last verse of the passage above in the "Modeling Jesus" section in chapter 2. However, there isn't a better verse to examine when discussing intimacy. It shows us the foundation of intimacy: *complete trust.*

One of the first things we see is that when Jesus is grieved, the first step He takes in processing His emotions is to share them with God. Unlike our husbands, our Father in heaven is always available with His time and emotions. So, when we need to share something that's on our hearts, let's turn to God, and then let's find space to let our husbands know we need to talk.

Next, we see Jesus requesting something from God. It's vital that we share our requests with God and with our husbands.

They need to know how we feel and our opinions; that's a huge part of intimacy! Finally, Jesus does something brave. He tells God that, above all, He desires the Father's will to be done.

No matter how frustrating intimacy can be in a military marriage, may we trust God's will to lead us into and out of situations that will mature us and sculpt us into image bearers of Christ. As I say this, remember that if what's happening in your marriage does not align with the loving heart of God and His Word, then it is not of God.

--------- *Prayer* ---------

Dear Lord,

Thank You for the gift of intimacy You gave us in marriage to reflect Your love for us. Because of our military lifestyle, intimacy often feels complicated or impossible to achieve. Please help me listen to the Holy Spirit's leading on cultivating ways to develop intimacy in my marriage. Soften my husband's heart, Lord, so he is also interested in discussing this topic and maturing in this part of his life. Please guide us to the right biblically and clinically informed counselor or program to help us if or when we need outside assistance. Clarify in my heart and mind why You designed marital intimacy and how to be a mirror image of Your love. And please do the same for my husband, God, drawing him intimately close to You and Your Word. In Jesus's precious name, amen.

——————————— *Reflection Questions* ———————————

1. On a scale of one to ten, with one being the least intimate and ten being the most intimate, where would you rate your current marital intimacy with your husband?

1   2   3   4   5   6   7   8   9   10

2. What improvements do you want to see in your marital intimacy?

3. Is there anything you're currently doing to hinder your marital intimacy?

4. Is there anything your husband is doing to hinder your marital intimacy?

5. Are there any past hurts between you and your husband that need to be processed so you can move toward healing and reconciliation?

6. Have you ever sought professional help, or do you think it would be beneficial if you've never done it before? Explain.

——————————— *Next Steps* ———————————

❑ Make a plan to talk about your marital intimacy with your husband and discuss topics from this idea and/or other related resources on intimacy.

❑ Find a biblically and clinically informed counselor if needed.

❏ Choose a marriage course, book, podcast, or conference from which you and your husband can continue your marriage education. If educating yourselves feels difficult right now, turn back to the enticing ideas listed earlier in this chapter for motivation.

—————————— *Resources* ——————————

For links and descriptions of each resource, visit Ashleyashcraft.com/missionreadymarriage.

- Emotionally Healthy Relationships Course
- *Passion Pursuit* by Dr. Juli Slattery and Linda Dillow
- *Intimate Issues* by Linda Dillow
- *Our Bodies Tell God's Story* by Christopher West
- *Unwanted* by Jay Stringer
- *Happily Even After: Let God Redeem Your Marriage* by Dannah Gresh
- *Fight for Love* by Rosie Makinney
- *The Seven Principles for Making Marriage Work* by John M. Gottman
- *Boundaries in Marriage* by Henry Cloud and John Townsend
- *Enjoy!* by Joyce and Clifford Penner
- *Quenched* by Jessica Harris
- *Stop Being a _____ Wife* by Ashley Ashcraft

- *Java with Juli* podcast
- *Lifegiver* podcast
- *Married to Military* podcast
- *Hearts & Stripes* podcast
- Dr. Jennifer Degler's website and resources
- The Association of Partners of Sex Addict Trauma Specialists
- International Institute of Trauma and Addiction Professionals

Chapter Twelve

Military Trauma: Coping with the Effects of War, Training, and Daily Operations

List the name of a fallen service member
you know and say a prayer for their
family: _____.

"You need to get help for me to stay in this marriage. I can't continue to do this." I desperately spewed these scary words a few months after my husband returned from Afghanistan. Knowing what I do now about combat trauma, I would have handled Tim's unfamiliar behavior *much* differently. It wasn't wrong for me to ask him to seek help, but grace and compassion were absent in my understanding and approach.

Despite the Army's efforts to educate me while my Soldier was deployed, I remained ill-equipped for reintegration after war. Tim agrees that he was also ill-equipped when he returned from deployment, both to reintegrate into our marriage and to recognize changes within himself. As a result, he didn't think there was a problem. And that's where the enemy saw an opportunity.

You see, trauma from war does not die on the battlefield; it may slowly seep out of the cracks in your husband's flesh or break down your front door with a sledgehammer. If our service members don't lose their life on the battlefield, Satan employs his destructive devices to claim victory at home.

When Tim returned from war, I viewed *him* as the problem instead of Satan, who was diligently using combat trauma to try to destroy my marriage. Remember, the enemy's primary goal is to steal, kill, and destroy (John 10:10). Second, some of Tim's PTSD symptoms triggered my own unprocessed trauma. As a result, both of us were frightened and confused walking through this unknown territory during our second year of marriage.

Thankfully, Tim reached out to his unit chaplain and discussed my concerns about him after returning from a war zone where he was shot down and lost close friends in his unit. While he did that, I confided in Christian friends and a Bible study leader at our church.

During Tim's next deployment to Afghanistan, a fellow military spouse whose husband was also dealing with PTSD symptoms suggested we work through a study called *When War Comes Home*. This manual is an essential tool every military wife needs! It opened my eyes to what Tim was experiencing and how I should care for my marriage, my husband, and myself amid combat trauma. I wonder how different our first reintegration would have been had I known about this resource.

If you're a new military wife or your husband hasn't been to combat, please don't write off this chapter as irrelevant.

Military-related trauma happens both at home and abroad. In fact, more troops are injured or killed during training exercises than in combat operations. We hate to think about it, but it's the truth.

According to the U.S. Department of Defense, from 2006 to 2021, 73 percent of U.S. troop casualties occurred by events unrelated to war. Delving deeper, 32 percent were accidents, 25 percent were self-inflicted, and 18 percent were due to illness or injury.[1] It is likely a matter of time before your husband gets deployed to a combat zone, loses a friend in training, experiences a military-related accident, or has to make a life-and-death decision. So highlight, make notes, and think of this as preparation. While you read, keep coming back to this verse about fear whenever you need it:

> "Do not fear, for I am with you; do not be
> afraid, for I am your God.
> I will strengthen you; I will help you;
> I will hold on to you with my righteous right
> hand." (Isa. 41:10)

What If My Spouse Never Goes to War?

There is the possibility that your spouse will never deploy to a combat zone. For you, I imagine that would be an answered prayer. For your spouse, however, that may be severely disappointing. Many of our service members signed up with a warrior mentality, ready to fight and defend their country. Never being able to put all their training into real-world action and earn a combat patch can leave a scar in its own right. A scar of unful-fillment. A scar of "wasted time." A scar of unworthiness. If your spouse struggles with the missed opportunity to serve in a combat zone, listen well, honoring his longing to serve.

Sarah, a fellow military spouse, is married to a service member who never had the chance to serve in combat. When the topic comes up in their marriage, she points out to her husband how he has made a difference in the military, even if not combat related. She encourages him by reminding him about the Soldiers he's assisted through hard times and the Soldiers' careers he's helped advance.

Sarah also aids her husband in recognizing how their marriage has grown due to his military service and how he has matured because of his time in the Army. She wants to help him see that his time in the armed forces hasn't been wasted because he didn't deploy to a combat zone, even if it may feel that way to him. What a beautiful example of love and encouragement Sarah provides for us!

What Is Trauma?

It wasn't until my adult years that the word *trauma* entered my vocabulary. Therefore, I didn't have a term to assign to some of the profoundly impactful negative situations I'd endured. Without the proper terminology and education on trauma, I assumed I needed to simply move on and get over the bad things that happened to me.

The problem is that's not how healing from trauma works. You cannot "just move on and get over it." In the book *Healing What's Hidden*, Evan and Jenny Owens, founders of REBOOT

Recovery, define *trauma* as "a deeply disturbing or distressing experience or series of experiences."[2]

The word *trauma* is a Greek word that means "wound." Throughout a lifetime, we'll all likely experience at least one traumatic event that results in our wounding, such as abuse, a natural disaster, a medical diagnosis, war, or an unexpected death of a loved one. Unfortunately, our husbands will likely be exposed to trauma much more than the average person due to the nature of their work, thus exposing us too.

During my husband's sixteen years in the Army, he has lost many military friends due to service-related deaths. Each time, traumatic details accompany the loss of someone he loves—a helicopter crash into a mountainside, a rocket that blew up the tent next to him where his coworkers were sleeping, and two aircraft that collided in midair. And these events do not include Tim's personal military-related traumas or traumatic experiences outside the service.

So, what happens to the brain when it experiences trauma, and why might trauma negatively affect your husband? Trauma literally *changes the brain*. If your husband returns from a traumatic deployment or training accident and acts differently, it's because his brain has actually *changed*. Please note this physiological change is out of his control; it's a natural response to trauma that changes the amygdala, hippocampus, and prefrontal cortex.

Due to this alteration, your husband's brain may no longer process information like before the trauma occurred. You may notice slowness in decision-making, outbursts over minor issues, fatigue, flashbacks, anxiety, and so on. These are initially normal responses to trauma that should decrease with healing. However, in some cases, when the brain struggles to process trauma, disorders may develop, causing an intensity, longevity, and expanse of symptoms.

The Spectrum of Traumatic Disorders

The military has a slew of names to assign to different disorders and reactions that may occur after trauma: Combat Trauma, Combat-Operational Stress Disorder, Deployment-Related Stress, Reintegration Issues, Acute Stress Disorder (ASD), and Post Traumatic Stress Disorder (PTSD). These terms are related but differ in severity. The most commonly discussed in our community is PTSD.

The Association for Behavioral and Cognitive Therapies (ABCT) defines PTSD as "distressing symptoms stemming from a traumatic occurrence that last longer than thirty days and interfere with normal life." ABCT lists the following sources of trauma for military personnel.

- Seriously injured people
- Dead bodies, human remains, or body parts
- Blast explosions (IEDs, mortars, rockets, rocket-propelled grenades)
- Mortuary duty
- Near misses
- Seeing others die
- Motor vehicle accidents
- Fearing for your own life
- Severely injured or ill medical patients
- Moral injuries (events that impact your moral values or beliefs)

- Hearing details or viewing images of traumatic events
- Sexual assault
- Physical assault
- Severe sexual harassment[3]

It's worrisome to read through the above list, but we must acknowledge what our spouses may face in this line of work and realize that the above list of traumatic events can happen during Garrison operations (at your local duty station) and while deployed. The above list is not combat specific.

There are four types of symptoms for those who struggle with PTSD. Although most people do not experience all the symptoms, they will have some in each category. As military wives, it's crucial for us to be informed so we can recognize these signs.

- *Reexperiencing symptoms:* Memories of the traumatic event that come out of the blue, dreams related to the event, flashbacks, or other intense distress when reminded of the experience.
- *Avoidance symptoms:* Avoiding distressing memories, thoughts, feelings, or reminders of the event.
- *Arousal:* Aggressive, reckless, or self-destructive behavior, sleep problems, being on guard, difficulty concentrating.
- *Negative thoughts and mood:* Blame of self or others, feeling cut off from others, loss of

interest in activities, inability to remember
important parts of the event.[4]

In some cases, even though your husband may be affected by
symptoms similar to PTSD, he may actually have a Traumatic
Brain Injury (TBI) or both. Many of the symptoms of PTSD are
also found in TBI cases, such as memory problems, sleep issues,
impulsivity, depression, isolation, and avoidance behavior.

According to Johns Hopkins Medicine, a TBI occurs when a
"sudden, external, physical assault damages the brain."[5] For our
service members, this often happens due to shock wave blasts
from an improvised explosive device, rocket-propelled grenades,
land mines, and projectiles like bullets, rocks, or fragments of a
fractured skull.[6]

Another factor in diagnosing and treating trauma is understanding that trauma goes beyond our mental and physical
selves. It also touches our souls. Evan and Jenny Owens ask this
wise question: "But what if some of the symptoms we experience
are evidence of a wounded soul rather than a wounded mind or
body? What if we've only been treating a portion of the problem?" They explain that "trauma wounds us in places that medicine won't reach and surgery can't touch. Trauma wounds our
souls. And these wounds need to be tended to . . . soul wounds
need a soul healer. And we believe the only one who can repair
a wounded soul is the original manufacturer—God himself."[7]

To help your husband seek God in the healing process, consider enrolling in a REBOOT Combat Recovery Course (something you can do as a couple) and providing him with a copy of
The Combat Trauma Healing Manual.

Seeking Help

In *Healing What's Hidden*, Jenny Owens states she quickly learned three things when she started working as a therapist on a military installation:

> You don't walk on the grass.
>
> You don't show up late.
>
> You don't tell the shrinks you're having mental problems.[8]

According to the Psychological Health Center of Excellence, 60–70 percent of military personnel with mental health symptoms do not seek care.[9] That number probably doesn't shock us because we know the potential consequences our husbands could face if they reveal mental health challenges, or so we've been told. Our heroes are trained to endure and sacrifice, so admitting "weakness" and needing help is entirely countercultural and requires deep humility.

Although there are several barriers to seeking help, such as lack of time, lack of confidence in treatment, lack of awareness of services, and negative attitude toward mental health, the primary barrier for our service members is stigma. The Defense Health Agency reports that 21 percent of service members and veterans fear they will be seen as weak, 32 percent believe their unit leaders would have a negative view of them, and 35 percent think seeking care would harm their career.[10]

Contrary to these popular beliefs, ABCT cites that "research suggests that over 95 percent of military personnel who voluntarily seek out mental health treatment from a military clinic do not experience any negative career impact." It's been noted that negative career impact is much more frequent among service members who refuse to seek treatment because they start having work-related problems. Prayerfully, our military personnel will begin to see that seeking mental health care early benefits their career (and their marriage!).

Unfortunately, as a military member, your husband likely has his own combat trauma story, or he will one day. According to historian Will Durant, there have only been 268 of the past 3,421 years when a major war wasn't raging somewhere on Earth.[11] In this lifestyle, it always feels like it's simply a matter of time before our husbands deploy. When we hear world news about war, we hold our breath and wonder if the military will call on our husbands to fulfill their oath to "defend the nation against all enemies, foreign and domestic." Due to the nature of their work, it only makes sense that many of our warriors would return with combat trauma.

To get a microscopic view of what our service members deal with after war, Jenny Owens shares a glimpse into the minds of the Soldiers she counseled (if graphic details about war are triggering for you, consider this your trigger warning and skip the rest of this section):

> One Soldier said, "Is it possible for my soul to die? I know I had one once, but now, when I look inward, all I see is a dark, black hole."

> "I stepped on the pressure plate. Why am I alive and he's dead? How do I look at his family, knowing I'm responsible?"

Another explained to her what it was like to watch the life leave the eyes of an Iraqi child he tried to rescue from a car bomb explosion.[12]

Not all military personnel need mental health treatment after combat stress, but many do, as you can understand from the examples above. Unfortunately, if appropriate care is not received, our service members and veterans may deal with the threat of suicide.

Suicide

In one of Tim's positions, he was responsible for filing SIRs (serious incident reports), so it was common for him to step away from dinner or playtime with the kids because of an emergency with one of the unit's Soldiers. Tragically, a few phone calls revealed a Soldier's death by suicide.

The military suicide rate is 57 percent higher than the national average.[13] That number is shocking. Yet, disturbingly, the statistic probably feels understandable because we see the stress and trauma our husbands and their units are forced to handle. In fact, suicide is the second leading cause of death in the U.S. military.

Even though we've primarily been discussing combat-related stress, it's crucial to understand that the effects of war are not the only cause of suicide among military members. ABCT cites that the most common stressors for military suicide and suicide attempts were relationship problems, legal issues, disciplinary problems, financial stress, and workplace difficulties. The organization also noted that service members with medical conditions like TBI, chronic pain, and sleep disorders were at an increased risk for suicide. The issue of military suicide doesn't end when someone's contract is fulfilled. Approximately twenty veterans die each day by suicide.[14]

In 2021, one of my dearest friends, Jennifer DeFrates (creator of Heaven Not Harvard and theMamapologist), called me with the news that her veteran husband, who endured several combat deployments and battled with TBI and PTSD, had taken his life. Because she has walked this road personally, I asked her if there was anything she wanted to share with you on this topic. Here are her insightful thoughts:

- Seek treatment aggressively. Our service members with PTSD and TBI are at an increased risk of suicide, and we have to advocate for their life.

- Suicidal behavior in veterans may not always look like the typical symptoms. Some things to watch out for are high-risk behavior, self-sabotage, and suicide by cop (when an individual chooses to perform an action that forces the police to use deadly force).

- Tell your husband that no matter how hard things are, you would rather fight through it with him than lose him.

- Praise your husband for everything you can.

- You will never regret loving him more than he deserves.

Reintegration after War

With all this heavy information on mental health in the military, it's natural to feel discouraged, maybe even defeated. I can hear some of you now: "Wow, Ashley, you really know how to bring a girl down. I feel more hopeless now than when I opened this book. Is it possible for my husband to leave the military healthy and alive?"

My answer? Yes, it's possible. In fact, I believe you and your husband can walk away from this military lifestyle stronger than you came into it *because* of the challenges you face in this community. The caveat is that God needs to be at the center of your lives, guiding and comforting you.

Next to putting God first, there are some practical steps you can take to equip yourself to handle the mental stressors of combat upon your husband's return.

- Read the book *When War Comes Home: Christ-Centered Healing for Wives of Combat Veterans*. Even if your husband has never deployed, the information you'll gain in this resource is key to your service as a military wife.
- Find a group of women (who follow Jesus) and do life together, supporting one another through the highs and lows of this lifestyle.
- Be open to seeking counseling or medical intervention if needed.
- Plan to offer your husband forgiveness and grace regularly.

- Provide space for him to grieve. Hopefully, he'll include you in the process. It is healthy for him to feel the emotions that accompany war.

Taking Care of Yourself

Do you remember what the word *trauma* means? That's right, "wound." If your husband experiences military-related trauma, you'll likely feel the pain of his wounds. Within any closely connected group, a person's trauma naturally touches those with whom they do life, especially within a family. So, as you help your husband care for his wounds, it's vital you take the time to care for yourself.

In some cases, military wives may experience Secondary Traumatic Stress (STS). In *Treating Compassion Fatigue,* Charles R. Figley describes STS as "distressing experiences of people who communicate at a deep level with someone who has been traumatized and become traumatized as well."[15] And who communicates more deeply with a service member than his wife? If you feel like you're experiencing symptoms of STS due to your husband's trauma, please seek help.

Here are several other ways you can care for yourself while you help care for your husband:

- Resting
- Involvement in your church community
- Reading God's Word
- Counseling
- Praying

- Physical exercise
- Eating healthy
- Sleeping
- Spending time with supportive friends
- Reading books about grief and trauma (to help you interpret any posttrauma emotions and to give you practical tools for responding to triggers)

Forgiveness (Not Permissiveness)

I pray that forgiveness is a regular rhythm in your marriage, a daily, moment-by-moment rhythm. We're all sinful human beings, and we all fall short of the glory of God (Rom. 3:23). Accepting that fact has helped my marriage dramatically because I no longer expect my husband to be a supersaint. (My husband likely scoffed at that last line, but I promise, I'm trying!) And I can release myself from the pressure to be perfect as well.

But when your husband returns from war or a training exercise, you'll probably get much more practice in the forgiveness department. It's the nature of reintegration. Two people are learning to live together again (more if you have kids), and it gets messy due to miscommunication, expectations, quirks, personal needs, and the demands of the military, which don't stop just because he returns.

Ephesians 4:31–32 is a powerful passage you can memorize to help you in moments that require forgiveness: "Let all bitterness, anger and wrath, shouting and slander be removed from you, along with all malice. And be kind and compassionate to one another, forgiving one another, just as God also forgave you in Christ."

If your husband comes back wounded (in mind, body, or soul), be prepared to grow in the area of forgiveness. On top of typical reintegration frustrations, he may display fits of rage, poor memory, substance abuse, emotional numbness, lack of interest, or an inability to trust. During these times, it's imperative to remember that your husband is not the enemy; Satan is. Your husband is made in the Almighty's image, dealing with a wounded soul. And if you're dealing with secondary trauma, the same goes for you!

Although forgiveness plays an essential role in the success of our military marriages, there is absolutely no room for abuse of any kind: verbal, emotional, physical, sexual, psychological, or spiritual. If your husband's war wounds cause him to abuse you or your children, you must seek help immediately and remove yourself from the home until it is safe to return. For help, you can contact your installation's Family Advocacy Program, chaplain, unit commander, law enforcement, or medical provider.

According to Scripture, condoning abuse is not loving or God honoring. You are not helping your husband, yourself, or your children by staying in a dangerous relationship. Removing yourself from an abusive environment allows you to find safety, and I pray it leads your husband to seek healing for his trauma wounds. (Sometimes natural consequences are exactly what a person needs to realize they have a problem and seek help!)

What If the Unthinkable Happens?

Yesterday, in preparation for my husband's new assignment, we had to fill out a form detailing how I would like the Army to handle my husband's death—something I don't want to consider. Questions ranged from how I would like the Army to notify me of his death, to if I wanted to meet his body at Dover Air Force Base, to the conditions in which I prefer to receive his personal belongings, and if I would allow media access.

Depending on your husband's branch of service or occupation, you may or may not be required to fill out a similar form. Whether or not you're faced with these questions on paper, consider working through this challenging topic with your spouse. Yet, regardless of your "preparedness," shock is always present when confronted with loss.

If the unthinkable happens, and two uniformed officers show up at your door or mine, I pray we make our way to trusting the Lord through the tragedy, knowing that grief will take us on a vast journey. Danita Jenae, my sweet friend, military widow, and author of the book *When Mountains Crumble*, received the knock we dread. Because I deeply admire how she candidly shares her grief journey and helps others rebuild their lives after losing a loved one, I asked for her guidance on this topic. Danita suggests that we surrender our husbands and their plans for their futures to the Lord in prayer now and ask God to strengthen our trust in Him and His plans. She leads us further by saying:

> As military spouses, we're forced to confront
> the possibility of our husband's death simply
> because of his rare occupation. Early on, I tried

to tackle my fears of losing my husband with God in prayer head-on. I eventually came to a place of trust and surrender, determining to bless the Lord who gives and takes away, regardless of my circumstances. I'm so grateful I wrestled with those fears with God years before my husband died because it put me in a more stable place mentally and spiritually when I got the knock on the door than if I had just tried to ignore or shove down those fears all along. I had already wrestled and dealt with many of my fears of losing my husband in prayer with God (as best I could) before it ended up actually happening to me. It didn't lessen the agony of losing Dan, but pre-positioning my heart toward trusting God no matter what did help me survive the agony and keep my faith in the Lord through it.

Sadly, Danita is not the only friend I know who has lost her husband in the military. After watching several of my friends endure this type of loss, I've observed that community is *essential* after notification of death. Unfortunately, Danita informed me that widows lose over 75 percent of their community within the first couple of months and not by their own choosing.

After the loss of a loved one, they need someone to hold them, to listen to them, to be present and yet say nothing, to clean their house, to care for their children, to drive them to appointments, to help them fill out paperwork, to pick up groceries, to make meals, to pray for them, and to step in wherever a need is seen. They need community.

Supporting Gold Star Families

Tragically, not every service member will return home from a deployment, training exercise, or daily operation. When a member of the armed forces dies in service to their country, their immediate family is known as a Gold Star Family. As I mentioned above, I believe it's imperative that we step in to love and serve these families. As God calls us to do, we need to look out for the needs of the widows around us. If a service member's death occurs in your unit, church, or local community, be ready to serve in love—in the immediate aftermath (if they permit you) and the long term.

Modeling Jesus: Handling Trauma with Care

What does it look like to genuinely love our wounded warriors in a way that emanates the heart of Christ? In a way that doesn't pass judgment? In a way that freely sacrifices for the benefit of our husbands? For that, we can look to the story of the good Samaritan.

In Luke 10, an expert in the Jewish law asked the Messiah what he must do to inherit eternal life. When Jesus asked the man his thoughts, the expert quoted the Great Commandment saying, "'Love the Lord your God with all your heart and with all your soul and with all your strength and with all your mind'; and, 'Love your neighbor as yourself'" (v. 27 NIV). The first part is self-explanatory, but the second left the expert with a question, which Jesus answered with a symbolic story.

> But wanting to justify himself, he asked Jesus, "And who is my neighbor?"

Jesus took up the question and said, "A man was going down from Jerusalem to Jericho and fell into the hands of robbers. They stripped him, beat him up, and fled, leaving him half dead. A priest happened to be going down that road. When he saw him, he passed by on the other side. In the same way, a Levite, when he arrived at the place and saw him, passed by on the other side. But a Samaritan on his journey came up to him, and when he saw the man, he had compassion. He went over to him and bandaged his wounds, pouring on olive oil and wine. Then he put him on his own animal, brought him to an inn, and took care of him. The next day he took out two denarii, gave them to the innkeeper, and said, 'Take care of him. When I come back I'll reimburse you for whatever extra you spend.'

"Which of these three do you think proved to be a neighbor to the man who fell into the hands of the robbers?"

"The one who showed mercy to him," he said.

Then Jesus told him, "Go and do the same." (Luke 10:29–37)

In this parable, we see the horrific treatment of a man whose traumatic experience left him "half dead" on the road. As a military wife, sadly, you may be able to relate to seeing your husband in a similar state. Even though he may have come home alive from war or combat training, it's possible that he feels half dead emotionally, spiritually, mentally, or physically.

So, what will we do if our husbands come home wounded? Let us not be like the first two people in the story, who *chose* to "pass by" the wounded man. We cannot ignore our spouses' pain; doing so may lead to irreversible tragedy. Think about it; the longer this man is left alone—stripped, beaten, and left for dead—will he get better? No, he'll get worse. Bones heal crooked and wounds get infected when left unattended. Instead, like Jesus (represented by the good Samaritan in this story), we must approach our husbands with compassion, provide them with extravagant attentiveness, and lead them to help.

When we show up in these ways, our husbands will experience the love of a merciful neighbor. Will we be wives who stop our agenda to care for our husbands (as the good Samaritan diverted his journey to care for the wounded)? Will we be wives who use our resources to bring healing to our husbands (as the good Samaritan spent his money and time to help the hurting)? Will we be wives who go to extraordinary measures in the care of our husbands (as the good Samaritan offered to reimburse extra expenses of the man's care)? And will we be wives who "come back" when the effects of woundedness may separate us emotionally (as the good Samaritan promises to return)? As women seeking to prioritize marriage and the Messiah, I trust we will.

———————————— *Prayer* ————————————

Dear Heavenly Father,
Thank You for the knowledge that while my service member may experience changes due to trauma, I can find hope in Your

unchanging nature. You are always good, always faithful, always trustworthy. Even though I may not understand why my husband and I must endure the effects of military trauma, please help me find peace in the truth that You work all things for good for those who love You (Rom. 8:28). I believe You will redeem any traumatic experiences and that we can partner with You to help others overcome their challenges with trauma. Please show me how to model Jesus as I care for my husband's wounds, and guide me as I strive to live a life that freely offers forgiveness. Thank You for the forgiveness You offer me day after day. In Jesus's forgiving name, amen.

Reflection Questions

1. Have you previously received education about combat trauma? If so, what was the source, and was it helpful?

2. List your fears about possible future deployments here and then release them to God in prayer.

3. If your husband has previously served in combat, how did his experience at war affect your marriage when he returned?

4. What are some ways you can take care of *yourself* if your husband ever deals with military-related trauma?

5. List the names of people or organizations you can contact if you ever need help for your marriage or your safety.

6. Is forgiveness something that comes easily to you or something you need to work on? Explain.

Next Steps

❑ Seek biblically and clinically informed counseling.

❑ Look online for a complete list of PTSD and TBI symptoms.

❑ Ensure you establish a loving group of local friends so you have a support system in place to help you through any challenges.

❑ Discuss with your family how you can support Gold Star Families.

❑ Pray Psalm 91 over your spouse.

Resources

For links and descriptions of each resource, visit Ashleyashcraft.com/missionreadymarriage.

- *Combat Trauma Healing Manual* by Chris Adsit
- *When War Comes Home* by Chris and Rahnella Adsit and Marshéle Carter Waddell
- *When Mountains Crumble* by Danita Jenae
- *The Body Keeps the Score* by Bessel Van Der Kolk, MD
- *Healing What's Hidden* by Evan and Jenny Owens
- *Faith Deployed* by Jocelyn Green
- *Sacred Spaces* by Corie Weathers

- *Down Range: To Iraq and Back* by Bridget C. Cantrell
- *Failure to Scream* by Robert Hicks
- *Triumph over Trauma* by Gregory L. Jantz, PhD
- *Indivisible*, the film
- REBOOT Combat Recovery course
- Yellow Ribbon Reintegration Program
- Armed Services Ministry—Never Alone
- USA Cares
- PTSD Foundation of America
- National Center for PTSD
- Veteran's Service Alliance
- 988 (Suicide and Crisis Lifeline)
- Stop Soldier Suicide
- Mighty Oaks Retreat
- Mentoring Our Military Code of Support
- Caregivers on the Homefront
- Team Red White and Blue
- Hope for the Warriors
- Give an Hour Mental Health Care
- Wounded Warrior Project
- The Warrior's Journey
- Hidden Heroes
- Psycharmor Caregiver Coursework
- Help for Our Heroes
- Viribus
- Detox Rehabs
- Legacies Alive
- Warrior Adventure Quest

Chapter Thirteen

Life after the Military: Figuring Out Your Next Chapter

Record your feelings about
leaving the military in one
word: _____.

"Give me twenty, and I'll give you the rest!" From the day we signed our marriage certificate in an antiquated town hall office in New York, that's been Tim's promise to me. He still tosses that phrase around jokingly when people ask how many more years he has in the service.

This sacrificial life regularly leaves me aching to depart as my flesh longs for comfort, ease, and the ability to choose. I'm tired of being told where I must live, when I have to leave, and allowing someone else to determine if my husband comes home or has to serve in another part of the world for weeks or months without seeing us.

Yet (and this is a big *yet*), the lessons I've learned about following Jesus in this sacrifice-inducing lifestyle are unparalleled. Where else would I have learned what it looks like to obey fully, regardless of my emotions? When the military orders us to move, I don't have the choice to tell the Army, "No, I don't *feel* like moving." I have to pack up and go where they say when they say. Period.

I can't help but compare that to how we should follow God. What if we said "Yes!" to every situation and place God called us to? Instead, we often shy away because of fear, the unknown, or unbelief in our abilities. I pray we can trust God regardless of our feelings. We can do this more readily than with the military because God cares about how we feel and welcomes us to share our qualms. In His love, He allows us to *choose* if we will obey.

Although the military trains us to follow orders, there's a time when that will cease and we will once again choose our next path. I'm repeatedly told it's a challenging transition to leave the military—for the whole family. There's a loss of identity, purpose, and community. So, how do we prepare ourselves to handle the transition out of the military well?

Deciding to Leave

Various reasons lead to exiting the military: retirement, ETS (expiration term of service), medical retirement, aging out, not being picked up for promotion, or an offense that leads to chaptering out. Some of these provide a choice, and others are decided for you. If you have a say in the matter, seek God's will about the right time to leave the military.

But what does "seeking God's will" look like? It can seem so vague and intangible. Discovering what God has for you starts with prayer and reading the Bible. In Hebrews 4:12, God tells us, "For the word of God is living and effective and sharper than any double-edged sword, penetrating as far as the separation of soul and spirit, joints and marrow. It is able to judge the thoughts and intentions of the heart." This means God's Word will "leap off the page" for us as we read. It can penetrate our hearts and reveal things to us.

You may not receive a clear answer. It would be so comforting to open the Bible and read, "Thus the Lord says, leave the military." But that verse isn't in there. Many times, reading the Bible won't give you exact specifics on what final call to land on when facing the ordinary decisions of daily life, but reading the Bible *does* make you a more discerning person over time, which will set you up to sense when it's time to go (or stay). So, as we immerse ourselves in God's Word over time, we will also pray, pray, pray, and then do our best to honor God with our choice by weighing all the pros and cons, considering the gifts He's given us, our finances, health issues, and family situation. However, God *may* give you a clear revelation on staying or leaving. If that happens, I encourage you to follow His command (even if you don't want to)! There's a reason He gave it to you; you don't want to miss what He's up to.

Making the Plan

Before our husbands leave the military, they'll have to go through a transition assistance program designed to equip them and their families with various resources for a successful transition into the civilian world. These programs educate our military members on veteran benefits, education options, employment, and federal assistance. (You can attend these classes with them!) Rest assured that the military is attempting to do its part to equip your service member for civilian life before he departs.

Although the military will prepare your husband for exiting the service from their standpoint, there's much to decide as a family. The decisions you must make can feel profoundly overwhelming, especially when your family is used to being told where to go, what to do, and when to do it. Ask God to help you make these decisions as a team and peaceably. Remember, you and your spouse are on the same team. The enemy will try to divide you, but hold fast to your husband and God's truth.

On the lighter side, Vicki Terrinoni, author of *Where You Go I'll Go,* says the best advice they received while planning retirement was for her husband to take six months off before jumping into another career or job. If it's financially plausible, embrace this advice to help ease the transition and enjoy some R&R time together as a family. You've *all* earned it!

Choosing Where to Settle

We have always planned to go home to the blistering hot desert of Tucson, Arizona, when Tim hits the twenty-year mark. Since both of our families live there, it seems like the obvious choice. But as the years to retirement grow shorter, God may lead us in another direction.

Tim loves our home and community near Fort Liberty. We enjoy the short two-hour drive to the beach, and with our child's recent Down syndrome diagnosis, we're near a top-ranked children's hospital. Considering all that and more, Tim recently said, "Maybe we should live here forever." I laughed because Tim was severely disappointed when we first received orders here.

In choosing where to live after the military, here are a few factors to consider:

- Job market
- Your family goals
- Housing costs
- Medical care
- Schools
- Church options
- Extended family
- Hobbies
- Areas in which you enjoy serving

Spend time in prayer asking God to lead your family in this decision, but know that He may not provide a clear answer. You can still make a wise choice on your own. We're so accustomed to being told where to go (and understanding that it's only temporary if we don't like it) that choosing where to live when we get out seems overwhelming. What if we choose the wrong state? What if we don't like our new home? What if our civilian jobs are unfulfilling?

The good news is that we're familiar with change. If your initial plan when leaving the military doesn't work out, we can adapt and try again. Your first plan out of the military doesn't have to be your forever plan. One of our friends moved to their dream home in Florida after retirement. Then, they decided to move to Pennsylvania to be near their family. Now, they call North Carolina their home. Maybe the itch to move just stays in our bones! Or maybe you'll love your first choice and stay settled forever. Breathe. It'll be okay. God has you wherever you go.

Finding Your Way in Civilian Life

If you have retirement pay, the Lord may lead you to a humbler position because you have that financial cushion. This was true for a recently retired Air Force pilot who felt the Lord calling him to pastor a country church in New York. Because he was financially stable due to his retirement pay, he didn't need to worry about the church's minimal budget and could serve where the Lord led him. Or, on the flip side, the Lord may lead you or your service member to a prominent position somewhere you didn't expect. In the end, "success" for the next chapter in your vocational journey isn't defined by the position itself; it is simply defined by saying yes to whatever door God asks you to walk through.

Think about your gifts, talents, and passions, along with what recent circumstances and opportunities God has brought into your life. One of my friends is a few years out from retirement and recently started offering respite care for foster families and volunteering. It's probably not a coincidence that God is leading her to serve in those areas shortly before she's ready to begin the next stage of her life out of the military.

Plugging into a New Community

For those who choose to live in a town without a military installation, losing our military community can be the most challenging part of this transition. My friend Kara shared these honest remarks on the topic:

> We were in Montana looking at property, and there I was, standing in a beautiful pasture, with amazing mountains all around me, long-horns on the property next door, God's beautiful creation all around me, and I had a panic attack. I felt like I was suffocating. I felt the sudden loss of a community and being alone. I wasn't expecting to feel like that at all. What would I do without women around me who knew what this life and these unique bonds of friendship were like?

If you relate to Kara, staying nearby a military community when you leave the military may be an easy answer. But if you can't, I encourage you to find or create a community wherever you settle. You can experience the benefits of a close-knit group by joining or starting a Bible study, a book club, a monthly mom's night out, a hobby group, or something similar. Wherever you end up, you need an intimate community to support you and whom you can serve. It's how God wired us!

Adjusting to Civilian Life

In an article on the military site Task & Purpose, Justin Nassiri writes that after interviewing more than fifty veterans, he noted the following:

Nearly every veteran I interviewed failed to anticipate the dramatic change in their personal finances when they left the military. Many of the most successful vets took pay cuts to prove themselves and work their way to the top, or took months longer than they anticipated in their job search to hold out for their ideal opportunity. Universally, they faced a steep learning curve when it came to new realities like taxable income, cost of living, medical insurance or utilizing veteran benefits.[1]

Although there will be practical adjustments like finances and insurance, we must also prepare for the emotional aspect of adjusting to civilian life. For many, leaving the military causes a significant sense of loss—a loss of not just income but community, support, identity, connection, friends, and service. Grieve that loss. Allow yourself to mourn. But I encourage you not to stay there. Embrace the new season God is leading you toward.

Continuing to Serve the Military

Knowing that God determines our boundaries, it's no accident that our families ended up in the military. Just because our time in the service is over doesn't mean it's time to stop serving the military community (potentially). Pray about this and seek God's will for your family. If God is calling you to invest in the military community beyond your service years, there are a myriad of ways you can obey this call—even if you're no longer getting paid by Uncle Sam. Here are a few suggestions:

- Attend or teach a Bible study on or nearby a military installation to encourage younger military spouses.
- Serve in the military ministry at your church or start one if none exists.
- Lead a REBOOT Combat Recovery Course in your community. (Veterans live everywhere!)
- Mentor a younger military spouse.
- Work or volunteer for an organization that serves the military.
- Participate meaningfully on holidays (i.e., place flags at a veterans cemetery on Memorial Day, attend a patriotic concert on Independence Day, or help your kids write Christmas cards to deployed service members).
- Ask the chaplain at a nearby military installation if there are ways you can volunteer to help cultivate spiritual growth for the service members and families in that location.

Knowing Your Identity beyond the Military

In 2022, I attended a Christian writers and speakers conference in Michigan called Speak Up. A day before the conference started, military spouses from around the country gathered for a special one-day training. Several women there were no longer active-duty spouses and struggled to explain their place in the community. Others reassured them with this phrase: "Once a military spouse, always a military spouse!" I loved witnessing the immediate inclusion and recognition of these women whose husbands had previously served.

However, many military spouses have expressed experiencing an identity crisis when their husbands leave the military. For so long, they rooted their lives in service to our country and this community that they no longer know who they are and where they fit outside the armed forces. I pray that the opposite is true for you.

I pray that you now know who you are *because* of your God-given time in the military. I pray that you acknowledge God put you here, in the military, with your unique gifts and talents to love and serve this community. I pray you allow Him to shape you in the adversities, understanding that He's molding you more and more into a reflection of Jesus. I pray that you learn to trust Him despite the perpetual trials. I pray you learn to lean into God's direction for you, following His plan for your life. I pray that when your time in the military is over, you see yourself clearly, as a beloved child of God placed here to delight in Him and glorify Him. You're so much more than a military spouse.

Advocating for Your Husband

The military will forever be a part of your husband's story, for better or worse. I hope he'll leave with positive memories of the camaraderie, hysterical stories that leave him laughing so hard he cries, pride in his service to our country, and friends he calls family. However, he may also depart with trauma wounds that still require healing.

As much as the military tries to prepare our service members for a successful civilian life, the statistic on veteran suicide points to a significant gap in proper preparation and continued care.

Sometimes loved ones of suicide victims state they had no idea their family member was hurting. So have the hard conversations. Make a point to discuss military trauma wounds with your husband and adamantly help him seek care! Let him know you're on his team and will do whatever it takes to get him help.

Just because his service in the military has ended doesn't means his wounds are healed. In fact, separation from what he's known so well may cause additional issues. That, coupled with the intense halt in the misson-ready pace of military life, will likely provide space for him to slow down enough to feel potential trauma, maybe for the first time.

He may also experience the effects of an identity crisis, not knowing where he fits in with society. Depending on his new job, he might feel he's no longer contributing meaningfully. And leaving his community of brothers and sisters in arms may leave deep holes. Be present, available, and in tune with your spouse's actions and emotions during this transition. He needs you.

Modeling Jesus: Returning to Teach and Serve

After Jesus's horrific death on the cross, He didn't call it quits here on Earth, retreating to the glory of heaven and glad to be over with His commitment here. He may have finished the job of the cross, but that didn't mean He hid away from human civilization forever.

He returned.

He taught.

He served.

In John 21, Jesus appears to His disciples for the third time since His resurrection, returning to visit them on the shore.

Greeting them during an unsuccessful fishing excursion, He told them where to find fish, and they hauled in an extraordinary number. When they made it back to land, they were greeted by a breakfast of fish and bread that Jesus had prepared for them. He returned. He taught. He served.

After that, Jesus provides healing and restoration to Simon Peter, allowing him to proclaim his love for Christ after denying that he was Jesus's follower three times.

> When they had eaten breakfast, Jesus asked Simon Peter, "Simon, son of John, do you love me more than these?"
>
> "Yes, Lord," he said to him, "you know that I love you."
>
> "Feed my lambs," he told him. A second time he asked him, "Simon, son of John, do you love me?"
>
> "Yes, Lord," he said to him, "you know that I love you."
>
> "Shepherd my sheep," he told him.
>
> He asked him the third time, "Simon, son of John, do you love me?"
>
> Peter was grieved that he asked him the third time, "Do you love me?" He said, "Lord, you know everything; you know that I love you."
>
> "Feed my sheep," Jesus said. (John 21:15–17)

Can you imagine the shame Simon Peter must have felt as he denied his relationship with Jesus because He feared enduring the same fate as Christ? I spent years denying the significance of my role as a military wife. I just wanted it to go away so I could live an easier life. (And I'm sure when our time is up in the military and the job is done, the enemy will tempt me to hole away in my home and avoid the needs of humanity all around me, using the excuse that *we've done plenty already*). But thankfully, Jesus invited me into a redemption story, just as He did with Simon Peter.

He asked me if I loved Him, if I was really ready to follow Him, to take His message of hope and truth, and to share it with others (to feed His sheep). And this time I said, "Yes, Lord. You know that I love You." That's why you're holding this book in your hands. I earnestly pray that after you've consumed these pages, you feel fed and full, satiated by the love of Christ.

Prayer

Dear Lord,

Thank You for the blessings you've bestowed upon me as a military spouse. Sometimes it's easy to see only the challenges, but there are also gifts. Yet You know more than anyone that this military lifestyle is confusing, exhausting, and sometimes debilitating. Through Your strength, please help me return to, teach, and serve the next generation of military spouses. Show me how to use my experiences and wisdom to benefit those behind me. Guide me in stewarding my military story well to lead other military spouses with hope, teaching them that You've placed them here for a reason. A grand, eternal reason: bringing healing and hope to the military community through the truth of Jesus. And Lord, when the time comes to transition out of the military, I also pray for Your guidance. Help us to seek You and Your will in all our preparation and decisions. Finally, I pray that when our military service ends, we recognize our identity is not solely as a military family. Help us find our worth and purpose in You. In Jesus's path illuminating name, amen.

Reflection Questions

1. Circle the number you identify with regarding your feelings about leaving the military.

   1   2   3   4   5   6   7   8   9   10

You'll have to drag me away physically!   It was good, but I'm ready to go.   Get me out of here!

2. What is your biggest concern about leaving the military?

3. When you leave the military, what will you miss the most?

4. Have you considered continuing to serve the military community after your time in service is complete? What are some ways you could help based on your interests and talents?

5. Do you think you and/or your husband might benefit from professional assistance after he leaves the military to help heal trauma wounds from his time in the service?

6. How would you define your identity outside of "military spouse"?

7. What are your gifts, talents, and passions? How can you use those to find purpose when you're no longer in the military?

Next Steps

❑ Attend transition classes with your husband
    when the time comes.

❑ Keep an open dialogue with your spouse about life after the military. Share your hopes and fears, and give space for both parties to communicate their highest priorities for the next chapter of life.

❑ After retirement/separation, plan a trip away and enjoy not having to request permission or report where you're going.

❑ Make a plan to pay off any debt before getting out of the military so it's an easier adjustment financially.

Resources

For links and descriptions of each resource, visit Ashleyashcraft.com/missionreadymarriage.

- Military OneSource
- Military.com
- The Military Wallet
- American Dream U
- Veteran.com
- Transition Assistance Program
- Veteran Career Fairs
- Hiring Our Heroes
- Hope for Warriors
- Instant Teams
- Credentialing Assistance Program
- Bunker Labs
- *Veteran Spouse Network* podcast

Tim's oath of office, 2007
(West Point, NY)

On the helipad after our
wedding ceremony, 2009
(West Point, NY)
(photo taken by Catherine Leonard,
used by permission)

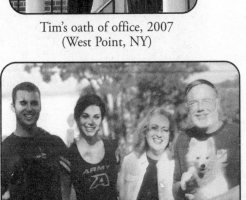

Our first neighbors,
Wally and Bunnie, 2009
(Belton, TX)

Tim's homecoming
ceremony, 2013
(Fort Bliss, TX)
(photo taken by Megan Urrutia,
used by permission)

Moments after Tim and Jake were
shot down, 2010
(FOB Salerno, Afghanistan)

Dumping our household
belongings due to mold,
2018 (Mountainville, NY)

Making our
12th move, 2020
(Fort Leavenworth, KS)

Tim's last flight in an Apache
helicopter, 2023
(Kitty Hawk, NC)

Our treasured blessing, Finley,
2023 (Duke Hospital, NC)

Our family, 2023
(Spring Lake, NC)

Notes

Chapter Two

1. Michael Rydelnik, John Hart, John Jelinek, John M. Koessler, Walter McCord, John McMath, William H. Marty, et al., *The Moody Bible Commentary* (Chicago, IL: Moody Publishers, 2014), 42–43.

2. Rydelnik et al., *The Moody Bible Commentary*, 43.

3. "Intention," *Merriam-Webster*, accessed August 19, 2023, https://www.merriam-webster.com/dictionary/intention.

4. "Agapaó," Strong's Concordance, Bible Hub, accessed August 19, 2023, https://biblehub.com/greek/25.htm.

Chapter Three

1. John Piper, *Desiring God* (Sisters, OR: Multinomah Books, 2018), 33.

Chapter Four

1. Adele Ahlberg Calhoun, essay in *Spiritual Disciplines Handbook: Practices That Transform Us* (Downers Grove, IL: InterVarsity Press, 2015), 245.

2. Emily Mailey, Carrie Mershon, Jillian Joyce, and Brandon Irwin, "'Everything Else Comes First': A Mixed-Methods Analysis of Barriers to Health Behaviors among Military Spouses," ResearchGate, August 2018, https://www.researchgate.net/publication/327044537 _Everything_else_comes_first_A_mixed-methods_analysis_of_ barriers_to_health_behaviors_among_military_spouses.

3. Arnold Cole and Pamela Caudill Ovwigho, "Understanding the Bible Engagement Challenge: Scientific Evidence for the Power of 4," Center for Bible Engagement, December 2009, https://bttbfiles.com/ web/docs/cbe/Scientific_Evidence_for_the_Power_of_4.pdf.

4. Caroline Leaf, "Why We Keep Making the Same Mistakes + Tips to Break Bad Habits," Dr. Leaf, May 9, 2019, https://drleaf.com/blogs/news/why-we-keep-making-the-same-mistakes-tips-to-break-bad-habits.

5. Annie F. Downs and Jeff Struecker, "Veteran's Day Conversation with Jeff Struecker," episode on *That Sounds Fun* podcast, no. 343, November 20, 2021.

6. "Would You Like to Know God Personally?" Cru, accessed March 5, 2023, https://www.cru.org/sg/en/kgp/would-you-like-to-know-god-personally.html.

7. Calhoun, essay in *Spiritual Disciplines Handbook: Practices That Transform Us*, 43.

8. Calhoun, essay in *Spiritual Disciplines Handbook: Practices That Transform Us*, 44.

9. Calhoun, essay in *Spiritual Disciplines Handbook: Practices That Transform Us*, 161.

Chapter Five

1. Kelsey Shade, "Dear Mama, Satan Would Move Heaven and Earth to Keep You from Reading This Letter," For Every Mom, April 23, 2020, https://foreverymom.com/faith/dear-mama-satan-screwtape-letter-kelsey-shade.

Chapter Six

1. Diana Juergens, *Wife of a Soldier, a Journey of Faith* (Columbia, SC: Self-published, 2018), 46.

2. Chuck Smith, "Verse by Verse Study on Matthew 12," Blue Letter Bible, accessed April 11, 2023, https://www.blueletterbible.org/Comm/smith_chuck/c2000_Mat/Mat_012.cfm.

Chapter Seven

1. Greg Laurie, "What Was the Great Commission and What Does It Mean for Us Today?" Christianity.Com, June 19, 2023, https://www.christianity.com/wiki/christian-terms/the-great-commission-is-the-great-command.html.

2. "Data," United States Military Spouse Chamber of Commerce, accessed June 22, 2023, https://milspousechamber.org/data.

Chapter Eight

1. "2021 Military Family Lifestyle Survey," Blue Star Families, accessed October 21, 2023, https://bluestarfam.org/wp-content /uploads/2022/03/BSF_Comp_Infographic_MFLS2021_03_10.pdf.

2. "A Message You Can't Afford to Be Silent On," Christian Stewardship Network, accessed October 21, 2023, https://www .christianstewardshipnetwork.com.

3. "Financial Health Statistics," Military Family Advisory Network, accessed August 17, 2022, https://www.mfan.org/topic /finances/financial-health-statistics.

4. "Strengthening Food Security in the Force: Strategy and Roadmap," Office of the Under Secretary for Personnel & Readiness, U.S. Department of Defense, July 2022, https://media.defense .gov/2022/Jul/14/2003035423/-1/-1/1/STRENGTHENING-FOOD -SECURITY-IN-THE-FORCE-STRATEGY-AND-ROADMAP.PDF.

5. Art Rainer, "Are Couples Really Divorcing over Money?" Center for Faith & Culture, August 27, 2018, https://cfc.sebts.edu /faith-and-economics/are-couples-really-divorcing-over-money.

6. http://www.ramseysolutions.com/dave-ramsey-7-baby-steps

Chapter Nine

1. BetterHelp Editorial Team, "How to Cope with Relocation Depression: Why Does Moving Make Me Feel Sad?" BetterHelp, July 4, 2023, https://www.betterhelp.com/advice/depression/relocation -depression-when-moving-makes-you-sad.

Chapter Ten

1. David Guzik, "Psalm 127—God's Work in Building House, Cities, and Families," Enduring Word, accessed October 21, 2023, https://enduringword.com/bible-commentary/psalm-127.

2. Paul Tautges, "The Refiner's Fire," Association of Certified Bible Counselors, September 18, 2020, https://biblicalcounseling.com /resource-library/articles/the-refiners-fire.

3. Charles Haddon Spurgeon, "Refined, but Not with Silver," The Spurgeon Center, January 1, 1970, https://www.spurgeon.org /resource-library/sermons/refined-but-not-with-silver/#flipbook.

4. Heather Avis, *Scoot Over and Make Some Room: Creating a Space Where Everyone Belongs* (Grand Rapids, MI: Zondervan, 2019), 35.

Chapter Eleven

1. Sam Yoon, "Yada—One of the Most Important Words for Your Marriage and Sex Life," Sam Yoon, February 2, 2015, https://www.samuelyoon.com/yada-one-of-the-most-important-words -for-your-marriage-and-sex-life.

2. Jonathan Petzold and Christa Petzold, "How Marriage Is a Picture of Christ and the Church," Concordia Publishing House Blog, June 7, 2021, https://blog.cph.org/read/how-marriage -is-a-picture-of-christ-and-the-church.

3. Yoon, "Yada."

4. Christopher West, *Our Bodies Tell God's Story: Discovering the Divine Plan for Love, Sex, and Gender* (Grand Rapids, MI: Brazos Press, 2020), 78–79.

5. Need source information.

6. Norica Vernon, "The Military Porn Problem," Proven Ministries, May 27, 2021, https://www.provenmen.org/the-military -porn-problem/#:~:text=Research%20shows%20that%20at%20 least,position%20is%20exempt%20from%20this.

Chapter Twelve

1. "Trends in Active-Duty Military Deaths from 2006 through 2021," Congressional Research Service, September 9, 2022, https://sgp .fas.org/crs/natsec/IF10899.pdf.

2. Evan Owens and Jenny Owens, *Healing What's Hidden: Practical Steps to Overcoming Trauma* (Grand Rapids, MI: Baker Books, 2022), 25.

3. "Military Post Traumatic Stress Disorder," Association for Behavioral and Cognitive Therapies, accessed June 22, 2023, https:// www.abct.org/fact-sheets/military-post-traumatic-stress-disorder.

4. "Military Post Traumatic Stress Disorder."

5. "Traumatic Brain Injury," Johns Hopkins Medicine, accessed June 22, 2023, https://www.hopkinsmedicine.org/health/conditions-and- diseases/traumatic-brain-injury#:~:text=What%20is%20traumatic %20brain%20injury,that%20happen%20to%20the%20brain.

6. Christopher B. Adsit, Rahnella Adsit, and Marshéle Carter Waddell, *When War Comes Home: Christ-Centered Healing for Wives of Combat Veterans* (Newport News, VA: Military Ministry Press, 2008), 19.

7. Owens and Owens, *Healing What's Hidden*, 77.

8. Owens and Owens, *Healing What's Hidden*, 21.

9. "Psychological Health Readiness," Health.Mil, accessed September 1, 2022, https://www.health.mil/Military-Health-Topics/Centers-of-Excellence/Psychological-Health-Center-of-Excellence/Psychological-Health-Readiness.

10. "Psychological Health Readiness."

11. Adsit, Adsit, and Waddell, *When War Comes Home*, 10.

12. Owens and Owens, *Healing What's Hidden*, 22.

13. Stop Soldier Suicide, accessed June 1, 2023, https://stopsoldiersuicide.org.

14. "Military Suicide," Association for Behavioral and Cognitive Therapies, accessed June 1, 2023, https://www.abct.org/fact-sheets/military-suicide.

15. Charles R. Figley, ed., *Treating Compassion Fatigue* (London: Routledge, 2002), 2–3.

Chapter Thirteen

1. Justin Nassiri, "5 Things No One Tells You about Getting Out of the Military," Task & Purpose, January 6, 2017, https://taskandpurpose.com/sponsored-content/5-things-veterans-dont-know-getting-civilian-job.